THE SATANISTS

The Satanists

Edited by

PETER HAINING

TAPLINGER PUBLISHING COMPANY
New York

First Published in the United States in 1970 by
TAPLINGER PUBLISHING CO., INC.
New York, New York

ISBN 0-8008-6995-8

Library of Congress Catalog Card Number 78-102068

Printed in the United States of America

For
AUGUST DERLETH
who could have
done it so much
better

INTRODUCTION

While it is undeniable that there has been a general increase of interest in fantasy and the macabre—perhaps owing to a certain desire on the part of war- and technology-weary men and women to escape the overwhelming presence of science and the machine—it seems to me manifest that curiosity about satanism has been stimulated in very large part by the book and film of Ira Levin's *Rosemary's Baby* and by Sybil Leek's *Diary of a Witch* and similar pieces, with all the attendant publicity accorded the self-vaunted witches of our own time.

As Mr. Haining points out in his introductory essay, witches are still practicing in our own day; we are no longer putting them to death, as in Salem, Massachusetts some centuries ago, but are inclined rather to send them to the nearest psychiatrist or to greet them with amused tolerance. There are covens in England, and there must surely be one or two in California, for every known kind of worship can be turned up there, and devil-worship is perhaps older than any sectarian rites rooted in the immediate past.

Satanism, however, is a rather more unpleasant kind of activity than we may have been led to believe by the kind of publicity afforded by the picture magazines, and the writers represented in Mr. Haining's anthology are well aware of it, and have been at some pains to bring home to the reader the terror and horror implicit in the shocking rites that might appear to the readers of the popular press as diverting or even somewhat silly.

Mr. Haining reveals, through the stories chosen for this

collection, something of the varieties of satanism, from the traditional view as in E. F. Benson's *The Sanctuary,* to the modern as in Robert Bloch's *Spawn of the Dark One.* These are popular tales for the most part, set beside actual accounts by, among others, such a lifelong authority as the Reverend Montague Summers, and by such an admitted practitioner as Aleister Crowley. They convey far better than the press reports, the deep-seated evil of satanism, they demonstrate that the age-old struggle between the benign and the malign is a never-ending one, and they illustrate beyond cavil the persistence of evil as well as the fascination evil holds for man.

—AUGUST DERLETH

CONTENTS

EDITOR'S NOTE

This is an anthology of fiction. The stories which you are about to read are all from the imaginations of top horror story writers —but in beginning the collection I have first stated (and set out to substantiate) the facts about Satanism being practised today—here in this country and very probably not far from your own home. I feel it is necessary for the reader to know a little of the background on which the majority of stories are based. My statements and conclusions are based on facts culled after patient and thorough investigation over a number of years. Though, as I have said, this is a collection of fiction— I would recommend you do not overlook the underlying fact that THE SATANISTS are abroad today—active in their pursuit of evil and degeneracy.

I have also included a factual report on the very pinnacle of the Satanists' practices—The Black Mass. It has been taken from the works of this century's most determined and knowledgeable foe of Satanism—the Reverend Montague Summers. During his life he investigated many fields of the occult and wrote several of the standard works on magic including the perennial best-seller *The History of Witchcraft and Demonology*. His statement on the Mass and its implications is a masterpiece of thorough research and enquiry.

Meet, now, THE SATANISTS—in fact and fiction. The dividing line is as narrow as you care to make it.

Black Mass
in a park starts police hunt

A group of people who celebrated a Black Mass with animals' hearts as sacrifices are being sought by police.

The police were called to a shelter at Malvern Park, near the centre of Solihull, Warwickshire, after an attendant found two hearts skewered to an altar improvised from park benches.

A crucifix was suspended upside down above it, and the altar was draped in mauve cloth. Burned candles were still there. Police took the relics away.

Chief Superintendent Dennis Fretwell, head of Solihull police, said: 'Inquiries are being made into ancient statutes concerning Satanism.

'We are most concerned about the motives of these people.'

The Sun
May 12th 1968.

Modern Satanism—the facts

PETER HAINING

It is an ordinary-enough-looking house in what is a typical London suburb. The red-brick front and neatly curtained windows look out across a carefully tended garden to a road parked with family saloon cars and a clutter of motorcycles and scooters. It is one of several hundred—all identical—that house a variety of city workers: clerks, accountants, cashiers and even a bank manager or two. Outwardly there is nothing to distinguish it from the others; inwardly it has been redesigned into something sinister and evil. . . .

The walls of the downstairs rooms are painted black and on them hang strange cabalistic signs made of silver and gold. In one of the rooms at the rear stands what is obviously an altar—on it is a skull and a cross placed upside down. Beside them lie a long pointed knife and a chalice which has obviously come from a church. On the floor alongside the altar—which is covered with a richly ornate black velvet cloth—stands a hideous goat mask. Two horns, one smeared with red paint, accentuate its repulsiveness. The thick, dark curtains at the french windows are drawn—they are always drawn. A thin ray of sunshine which has managed to find a way through a slight tear falls on a small table in the far corner. On it stands a large plastic bowl—the everyday kind which can be bought in Woolworth's or any other chain store for a few shillings. The bowl is full of blood. And a soggy, grey-coloured lump of matter not long cold.

The lump of matter is a sheep's brain.

The room is in readiness for a ceremony. A ceremony straight from the Dark Ages. A ceremony many people have erroneously believed to have died with the persecution of witches in the seventeenth century. A ceremony of evil and perversion.

The Black Mass.

In the space of just a few years Satanism has become a widespread evil throughout the length and breadth of Great Britain. From being the preserve of a few isolated cranks and sexual perverts, it has grown with alarming speed into a nationwide network with members from all strata of society. From the wealthy searching for new perversions to frustrated clerks, tormented office workers, factory hands, labourers—all are known to belong to the ranks of this black art.

And it is not just an occasional activity—the practice of the cult's sexual and sacrificial rites occurs as frequently as church services: the twentieth-century devotees of the Devil are disciplined and regular in their debased observances.

The presence of this cult is still, however, unacknowledged by the vast majority of people. Many are inclined to ridicule the very idea of Satanism. Others may grudgingly accept that it exists, but denounce all its practitioners as sexual perverts and ignore the creeping insidiousness of its beliefs. The few who treat it seriously as a growing evil have watched it slowly emerge from the underground in recent years with the more frequent discovery of abandoned altars complete with black candles and animal hearts and an increasing number of outrages in churches and cemeteries.

Who, then, are THE SATANISTS—and what are their beliefs?

Theirs is the most publicised, most attacked, most bestial, yet still the least understood secret sect in the country. More words have been written about Black Magic than probably any other subject, excepting Vietnam, politics and the Royal Family. It is regarded by newspapers as a circulation booster, though few of them ever put it in its right perspective and more often than not confuse it with a variety of other practices. It is also without doubt the most thoroughly evil organisation flourishing in Britain today.

It is a cult which imposes the strictest vows of silence on members—and metes out the most terrible punishments on those who disobey. It strips a man of his dignity and may frequently demand that he debase himself in the most sickening ways. It deprives a woman of her honour and allows her no morals whatsoever. It has even been known to force small children—boys and girls who have barely reached puberty—to take part in barbaric acts which most people believe have not been heard of since the fourteenth and fifteenth centuries.

It is an organisation dedicated to undermining the Church, outraging society and exploring any means for corrupting the authorities and government.

The covens of modern Satanists are known as The Fraternity of the Goat. As a general rule they foregather in groups of thirteen, though it is not unusual for the number to be much larger. Each coven is administered by 'The Goat' or High Priest, usually an elderly man who conceals his identity throughout all the rituals beneath a goat mask.

There are few set dates on which the devotees meet—they are usually governed by the availability of somewhere 'safe' to assemble. The meetings are called 'Sabats' and it is at them that the notorious Black Mass is performed.

There are, however, four dates on the calendar which are rigorously observed: February 2nd, June 23rd, August 1st and December 21st. Each of these days marks the start of the 'Sabats-in-Chief'—Black Magic festivals which can be equated in importance to Christmas and Easter.

The modern Black Mass is not, however, performed with the old idea of trying to conjure up the Devil in physical form. Today's acolytes do not believe there is such a being as the Devil, just as they no longer believe that the way to see a vision of Lord Satan is to smear one's face with the blood of a goat which has been boiled with vinegar and crushed glass.

They believe, quite simply, in the existence of evil as a *living force.*

That the faithful still pay lip-service to the idea of a Devil by honouring 'The Goat' during the ceremonies is a concession to the past. The Satanist taking this role represents, in a form they can all see, the many powers of evil.

Just how well established are the Satanists? There is documented evidence of their existence in no less than sixteen counties—and that number is, I believe, barely scratching the surface. My own estimate based on my enquiries is that the number of devotees runs into many thousands, the majority of whom have managed so far to keep their identities—and many of their nefarious activities—secret from the police and the authorities.

The covens recruit many of their members from among the weak-minded, the easily deluded and the sexually restless. Their best hunting grounds are the fringes of the Occult world and the esoteric groups where members have become dissatisfied with their 'progress' into the mysteries. The Satanists find it an easy task to convince these unfortunates of the 'better times' that lie ahead if they join them. And once they learn the sinister truths of this new group they have been introduced to, it is much too late to pull out. For as soon as the disciple has been initiated into the secrets of the cult, there is no intention that he or she should ever be allowed to pass on this information to others.

In cases where the victim does try to break away the simple hint of a beating-up may well quell such ideas. In others the threat of violence to family or relatives is required. While in extreme circumstances—where a man holds a position of trust or authority—blackmail may well have to be employed also. To an organisation which rejects all that is good and honourable, any ends justify the means whereby they can prevent their numbers being depleted or their dark secrets exposed.

Selected men and women are, of course, approached quite openly to join a coven—while extreme cases even apply. These people are often admitted after only brief enquiry into their lives—being known perverts who have already come to the notice of the leaders of the covens. In taking such steps these people often throw away their last chance of ever leading a normal life.

Much that has been rumoured about Satanism is true. And much more that has not even been guessed at. The covens *do* meet at dead of night and dance abandonedly in the nude. They *do* carry out blood sacrifices using live animals. They *do* perform diabolical acts of sacrilege, desecrating graves and wrecking churches. They even carry out terrible rituals with human beings . . . women being brutally raped and men flogged to the point of collapse. They are no strangers to death, either, and there are very good reasons for suspecting that Black Magic may have taken its toll of several lives within the last few years.

The Satanists, Devil Worshippers, Black Magicians—they are all one—are the modern practitioners of an evil ritual which goes back to the dawn of history. They are the descendants of those early, superstitious people who chose the Prince of Darkness in preference to the authoritarian church.

And in sheer malignancy, evil and perversion, the Satanists in 1969 have surpassed all previous generations.

As I have already intimated, the true Satanist is more than just someone who is 'kinky' or searching for bestial pleasure: a disciple must be capable of defying all that is good and prepared to waive any standards of decency he may have. He must be ready and willing to desecrate the most holy symbols of the Church and disqualify his soul from any chance of an afterlife.

But it is the final test before complete admission to the coven takes place which demands more than all the others. For the weak it is a sickening task that many flinch from; even for the strong it can be a trial which leaves them vomiting and ill.

The neophite is called upon to ritually kill a small animal—a bird or cat, perhaps—and then drink its still-warm blood. Finally, in full view of the members of the order, he must have intercourse with a selected woman. Young girl—or elderly degenerate—he has no choice. For a female disciple the same conditions apply—except that she must offer herself to as many of the men who want her.

Now the new Satanist is ready to be present at the greatest of all Black Magic mysteries—the Black Mass. The fearful ritual of evil and sadism, the ultimate in degeneracy.

It is at this point which I propose to conclude my own personal report on the modern Satanists and leave the floor to a man with a far deeper knowledge of the Black Mass than mine —the Reverend Montague Summers. His account which follows is a chilling, true statement which I hope will underlie the fact in the fiction which follows it.

In any case, enjoy the stories of THE SATANISTS—you can always close the book when darkness falls.

Finchley, London—
Broxbourne, Herts
1965–1969

The Satanic Mass

MONTAGUE SUMMERS

The great central act of Christian worship is the Mass, a Sacrifice which can be offered to God alone, but the climax of Satanism is the horror of the black mass, a sacrifice of mockery, impiety, and blasphemy which is offered to the Devil. Satanists today often meet with the celebration of the black mass as their main object, and it is indeed the culmination and—to use a term of the schools—the very quiddity of devil-worship and the cult of hell. In detail the black mass imitates, so to speak, and foully parodies with every circumstance of crapulous obscenity and contempt the Sacrifice of Calvary.

The black mass today is sometimes celebrated in a cellar, but Satanists have become so audacious and so strong in evil that the largest room in their house is known to be permanently fitted up for these abominable mysteries. In one case the room is draped with black hangings and the windows are always shuttered with curtains drawn. The fact that the door is furnished with Yale lock and key arouses no suspicion. Sometimes even a disused chapel is bought by a wealthy Satanist and furnished for the ceremonial of the liturgy of the pit.

The Abbé Guignard, a member of the La Voisin coven, chanted Satanic Masses in a cellar over the body of Marianne Charmillon; the Duc de Richelieu (1696–1788), who was, it is said, tutored in black magic by a disciple of the Abbé Guibourg, caused two friars, who were his chaplains, to celebrate black masses in the old deserted chapel of one of his country houses, a remote decaying château. He himself assisted with other devotees. Pierre Davis, Mathurin Picard, and Thomas Boulle, who were attached to St. Louis and St. Elizabeth, at Louviers, celebrated black masses at the sabbats which were held in some house not far from the convent, a rendezvous aptly termed a 'den of devils'.

I know of a black mass celebrated at night in a room at the back of a small, squalid shop in the slummiest part of Brighton not far from Brighton Station. At Merthyr Tydfil the black mass was said or sung in the basement back room of a little house in a poor street, where lived an old man who was reputed to be a 'fortune-teller', and who boasted that he belonged 'to the oldest religion in the world'.

This back room was furnished as a chapel, and the altar, above which was suspended a pair of queer-looking horns, whilst odd objects were ranged on the gradine, blazed with candles. Sometimes the altar is swathed in black velvet, and there are six black candles, three on either side of a crucifix. The crucifix is hideously distorted and caricatured, as J.-K. Huysmans saw at the black mass in the old Ursuline convent near the rue de Vaugirard. Mons. Serge Basset, who was taken to a black mass, observed that in the centre of the altar where a crucifix should be placed was squatting the monstrous figure of a half-human buck-goat, with staring eyes which flickered with red fire, whilst from the tips of its huge horns jetted a dull crimson flame. The altar table itself is generally covered with the three regulation fine linen cloths, overlying the cere-cloth of waxed linen. Sometimes a frontal of brocade or silk is used, and this has been known to be worked with designs of the most obscene esotericism, with many-rayed stars which had men's and women's faces, triangles twined with hissing adders, and the whole heraldry of hell.

In May 1895, at the Palazzo Borghese, which vast palace had been rented in various suites of apartments, a Satanic chapel was discovered, *Templum Palladicum*. The walls of the room were draped with scarlet and black curtains excluding all light; at the farther end was stretched a huge tapestry depicting

'Lucifer Triumphans', the Devil Triumphant, Conqueror of the World, and underneath an altar was erected, in the midst of which between the candles stood a figure of Satan to be adored by his worshippers. The room was furnished with luxurious prie-dieus, with chairs of crimson and gold, with tabourets and faldstools. It was lit by electricity, so arranged as to glare from an enormous human eye fixed in the middle of the ceiling.

The vestments worn by the hierophant of the eucharist of hell are often of the richest quality and embroidered with the most delicate workmanship, for the Satanists have immense wealth at their command. At the black mass witnessed by Mons. Serge Basset the celebrant was vested in an alb trimmed with richest lace and a cope of flaming scarlet covered with gilt pomegranates and cones. He wore scarlet silk shoes. The Abbé Guibourg was robed in an ample chasuble thickly sewn with occult characters wrought in silver. At a black mass of fairly recent date the priest wore a chasuble of the ordinary shape, but in colour a deep red and on the back was embroidered a huge triangle of some shimmering silk in the midst of which a black goat standing upright butted with his silver horns.

There have been described to me, by those who actually saw them, a chasuble of heavy orange satin with a he-goat worked in black; another chasuble was of a peculiar shade of brown, embroidered with a pig and a naked woman in delicate flesh-tint; a third was of a hard glaring scarlet adorned with an enamelled plaque of arsenical green on which were a bear and a weasel devouring the host. There was also a cope of exquisite grey silk on which was woven a female figure with buskined legs, wearing a short sky-blue tunic and the red Phrygian cap. The figure, which in one hand raised aloft a severed head streaming in blood, was surrounded by a garland of oak leaves, and beneath appeared the date '21 Janvier, 1793', the murder of King Louis XVI. The figure represented the Goddess of Reason, who attired in this garb was placed upon the high altar of Notre Dame in the person of a common strumpet, adored by the Revolutionaries and Parisian satanists.

For the order of his service the celebrant of the black mass uses a 'missal', which is sometimes a printed book, although more often a manuscript. Some of these 'missals' are written in red characters upon vellum. Madeleine Bavent speaks of priests celebrating the black mass, and 'reading from the Paper of Blasphemy'. These 'missals' are by no means the same as, but must be entirely distinguished from, grimoires and books of spells.

The host is generally black. In 1324, when investigation was being made into the sorceries of the famous Kilkenny witch, Alice Kyteler, they found hidden away in the lady's chamber 'a wafer of sacramental bread, having the devil's name stamped thereon instead of Jesus Christ'. The devil's host is often of grotesque shape, triangular, with three sharp points as used in the Mass of St. Sécaire, or hexagonal. In colour it is sometimes black, sometimes blood-red. Gentien le Clerc, a young satanist of Orleans, who was executed in 1614, 'had often seen the devil's priest elevate the host and the chalice, of which both were black'. At Rome there were discovered in a brothel two hosts scrabbled over with letters in human blood. These had been stolen from a church and were to be employed in a love-charm.

The thefts of consecrated Hosts from churches is a fearful profanity which has persisted throughout the ages and was never more common than today. The Host is stolen to be desecrated and abused by the Satanists at their assemblies, or it may be in private, secretly and alone.

Presenting themselves at the altar for Communion, these wretches retain the Host in their mouths and then unseen convey It to a handkerchief or handbag. There is a regular traffic in this kind of thing, and considerable sums of money are paid by those who will actually purchase Hosts secured in this way. Nor is it unknown for the Tabernacle of a church to be rifled during the night. A thief can ask his own price for the Reserved Sacrament, and can always find a ready market in certain occult circles.

This is nothing new. We are continually meeting with these abominations throughout the Middle Ages. Dan Michel, of Kent, writing in 1340, speaks of the abuse of the consecrated Host by witches and evil priests as an atrocious crime, but one unhappily known in former centuries. He also mentions the abuse of chalices which have held the Precious Blood. In 1410, when the Queen-regent Dona Catalina was at Segovia, there was discovered a hideous sacrilege, the maltreatment of the Consecrated Host by a band of Jewish sorcerers. They had also attempted the life of the Bishop of Segovia. The Jewish synagogue was converted into a church of reparation, Corpus Christi, and an annual procession still commemorates these events. In 1507 Martin Plantsch, denouncing witchcraft, deplores the magical masses and the profanation of the Host. In 1532 three Hosts were stolen on Good Friday from a church in Aldgate for black magic, as is recorded in the Chronicle of the Grey Friars. There was a terrible scandal in 1614 regarding the theft of numerous Hosts from the tabernacle of the Cathedral at Porto, and the Inquisitor in Portugal, Manuel Do Valle De Moura, issued particular instructions that the Host must be most securely kept under lock and key lest it be stolen for some hideous blasphemy of witchcraft. In July 1938, the Vatican published new rulings to protect tabernacles. These laws are most stringent and most detailed. Thus the tabernacle must be immovable, shut on all sides, and of solid material. The key must never be left in the door or on the altar. The employment of safety-alarms is urged to prevent attempts at stealing the Hosts. 'World-wide thefts of Sacred Hosts are responsible for the new legislation concerning the safe custody of the Blessed Sacrament. It has been known for many years that attacks upon tabernacles are not inspired by the value of the sacred vessels.'

There is cumulative evidence for these thefts and defilements during the past twenty, forty, seventy years. Indeed, so active in wickedness are the Satanists that scarcely a month passes without some such incident, some sacrilege, is reported.

So close is the mimicry of the black mass that, although the ceremony is actually no part of Holy Mass, the *Asperges*, the sprinkling of the clergy and congregation with holy water, is often burlesqued. Boguet tells how 'they say mass at the sabbat'. He who is to celebrate is clothed in a cope with no cross upon it—or sometimes a broken cross—and the worshippers are sprinkled by the Grand Master holding a black asperge with brackish water or even filthy chamber-lye.

Until modern times the burning of incense at the black mass is rarely noted, although there were mystic suffumigations in conjuring of evil spirits. Silvain Nevillon, a member of the Orleans coven (1615), described in detail a black mass at which he had assisted, when the place—it was held in a house—was thick and foggy with a smoke that smelled abominably, not fragrant and sweet as is the incense burned in churches. The witches brought Hosts which they had kept when feigning to make their Communions at various altars, and the Devil (the Grand Master) fouled the Hosts with fearful blasphemies. Water, or some stinking liquid, was scattered over those present, and the Devil chanted *Asperges Diaboli.* He seemed to read the liturgy from a book which was bound in shaggy skin like the pelt of a wolf. On occasion the Devil preached a sort of sermon, but he spoke in a low gruff voice and it was hard to hear what he was saying.

Today Satanists burn in thuribles and in braziers church incense during their hellish liturgy. They also make a kind of incense from various herbs and spices, the smoke from which is sometimes fetid and stale, sometimes languorous and swooning-sweet.

'Every action of the mass which I saw celebrated at the sabbat', confessed Madaleine Bavent, 'was indescribably loathsome.'

And so the travesty, the eucharist of hell, proceeds from blasphemy to blasphemy, from obscenity to obscenity, until the canon is reached, or rather the point corresponding to the

Canon of the Mass. Then 'the Host is really and truly consecrated and offered to the demon'. At this moment the celebrant turns his back to the altar.

In some modern assemblies, immediately after the elevation of the chalice there are distributed to the congregation smaller chalices or goblets of wine mingled with some potent aphrodisiac, and before long the scene is a saturnalia of indiscriminate and demented debauchery.

It has been remarked that the black masses of Giles de Rais at Tiffauges and Machecoul, masses said by the young Florentine sorcerer priest, Francesco Prelati, as also the masses said by the Abbé Cotton, by the Abbé Lemaignan, and by the Abbé Guibourg over the naked body of Madame de Montespan, were murderous as well as sacrilege, but whatever the black mass of the modern Satanist lacks in blood it amply makes up in blasphemy and bestial rut.

Yet, if what is whispered be true, and there seems strong confirmation enough, the shedding of blood is not unknown among the devil-worshippers today in London; in Brighton and Birmingham; in Oxford and Cambridge; in Edinburgh and Glasgow, and in a hundred cities more of the British Isles.

Witchcraft—black magic—Satanism, call it by what name they will, for it is all one, the cult of the Devil is the most terrible power at work in the world today.

There is probably no other writer of macabre literature more suited to opening a collection such as this than *E. F. Benson.* For he was the son of an Archbishop of Canterbury and while he never actually encountered Satanism in action, he was made very much aware of its existence through his father's work. Benson did not seek his own living in the Church, however, but turned to writing and during his life showed himself as a man of enormous literary talent and output. He had a lifelong interest in the Occult and produced several collections of ghost and horror stories—most of which are now sadly out of print. Never afraid of committing himself in print, he scandalised Victorian society with his first novel *Dodo* and then went on to turn many a delicate stomach with his gruesome weird tales. 'The Sanctuary' undoubtedly qualifies among the best of these and has certainly lost none of its power over the fifty-odd years since it was written.

The Sanctuary

E. F. BENSON

Francis Elton was spending a fortnight's holiday one January in the Engadine, when he received the telegram announcing the death of his uncle, Horace Elton, and his own succession to a very agreeable property: the telegram added that the cremation of the remains was to take place that day, and it was therefore impossible for him to attend, and there was no reason for his hurrying home.

In the solicitor's letter that reached him two days later Mr. Angus gave fuller details: the estate consisted of sound securities to the value of about £80,000, and there was as well Mr. Elton's property just outside the small country town of Wedderburn in Hampshire. This consisted of a charming house and garden and a small acreage of building land. Everything had been left to Francis, but the estate was saddled with a charge of £500 a year in favour of the Reverend Owen Barton.

Francis knew very little of his uncle, who for a long time had been much of a recluse; indeed he had not seen him for nearly four years, when he had spent three days with him at this house at Wedderburn. He had vague but slightly uneasy memories of those days, and now on his journey home, as he lay in his berth in the rocking train, his brain, rummaging drowsily among its buried recollections, began to disinter these. There was nothing very definite about them: they consisted of suggestions and side-lights and oblique impressions, things observed, so to speak, out of the corner of his eye, and never examined in direct focus.

He had only been a boy at the time, having just left school, and it was in the summer holidays, hot sultry weather of August, he remembered, that he had paid him this visit, before he went to a crammer's in London to learn French and German.

There was his Uncle Horace, first of all, and of him he had vivid images. A grey-haired man of middle age, large and extremely stout with a cushion of jowl overlapping his collar, but in spite of this obesity, he was nimble and light in movement, and with a merry blue eye that was equally alert, and seemed constantly to be watching him. Then there were two women there, a mother and daughter, and, as he recalled them, their names occurred to him, too: they were Mrs. Isabel Ray and Judith. Judith, he supposed, was a year or two older than himself, and on the first evening had taken him for a stroll in the garden after dinner. She had treated him at once as if they were old friends, had walked with her arm round his neck, had asked him many questions about his school, and whether there was any girl he was keen on. All very friendly, but rather embarrassing. When they came in from the garden, certainly some questioning signal had passed between the mother and the girl, and Judith had shrugged her shoulders in reply.

Then the mother had taken him in hand; she made him sit with her in the window-seat, and talked to him about the crammer's he was going to: he would have much more liberty, she supposed, than he had at school, and he looked the sort of boy who would make good use of it. She tried him in French and found he could speak it very decently, and told him that she had a book which she had just finished, which she would lend him. It was by that exquisite stylist Huysman and was called *Là-Bas*. She would not tell him what it was about: he must find out for himself. All the time those narrow grey eyes were fixed on him, and when she went to bed, she took him up to her room to give him the book. Judith was there, too: she had read it, and laughed at the memory of it. 'Read it, darling Francis,' she said, 'and then go to sleep immediately, and you will tell me tomorrow what you dreamed about, unless it would shock me.'

The vibrating rhythm of the train made Francis drowsy, but his mind went on disinterring these fragments. There had been another man there, his uncle's secretary, a young fellow, perhaps twenty-five years old, clean-shaven and slim and with just the same gaiety about him as the rest. Everyone treated him with an odd sort of deference, hard to define but easy to perceive. He sat next to Francis at dinner that night, and kept filling his wine-glass for him whether he wanted it or not, and next morning he had come into his room in pyjamas, sat on his bed, looked at him with odd questioning eyes, had asked him how he got on with his book, and then taken him to bathe in the swimming-pool behind the belt of trees at the bottom of the garden.... No bathing-costume, he said, was necessary, and they raced up and down the pool and lay basking in the sun afterwards. Then from the belt of trees emerged Judith and her mother, and Francis, much embarrassed, draped himself in a towel. How they all laughed at his delightful prudery.... And what was the man's name? Why, of course, it was Owen Barton, the same who had been mentioned in Mr. Angus's letter as the Reverend Owen Barton. But why 'reverend', Francis wondered. Perhaps he had taken Orders afterwards.

All day they had flattered him for his good looks, and his swimming and his lawn-tennis: he had never been made so much of, and all their eyes were on him, inviting and beckoning. In the afternoon his uncle had claimed him: he must come upstairs with him and see some of his treasures. He took him into his bedroom, and opened a great wardrobe full of magnificent vestments. There were gold-embroidered copes, there were stoles and chasubles with panels of needlework enriched with pearls, and jewelled gloves, and the use of them was to make glorious the priests who offered prayer and praise to the Lord of all things visible and invisible. Then he brought out a scarlet cassock of thick shimmering silk, and a cotta of finest muslin trimmed round the neck and the lower hem with Irish lace of the sixteenth century. These were for the vesting of the boy who served at the Mass, and Francis, at his uncle's bidding, stripped off his coat and arrayed himself, and took off his shoes and put on the noiseless scarlet slippers which were called sanctuary shoes. Then Owen Barton entered, and Francis heard him whisper to his uncle, 'God! What a server!' and then he put on one of those gorgeous copes and told him to kneel.

The boy had been utterly bewildered. What were they playing at, he wondered. Was it charades of some sort? There was Barton, his face solemn and eager, raising his left hand as if in blessing: more astonishing was his uncle, licking his lips and swallowing in his throat, as if his mouth watered. There was something below all this dressing-up, which meant nothing to him, but had some hidden significance for the two men. It was uncomfortable: it disquieted him, and he wouldn't kneel, but disrobed himself of the cotta and cassock. 'I don't know what it's about,' he said: and again, as between Judith and her mother, he saw question and answer pass between them. Somehow his lack of interest had disappointed them, but he felt no interest at all: just a vague repulsion.

The diversions of the day were renewed: there was more tennis and bathing, but they all seemed to have lost the edge of their keenness about him. That evening he was dressed rather earlier than the others, and was sitting in a deep window-seat of the drawing-room, reading the book Mrs. Ray had lent him. He was not getting on with it; it was puzzling, and the French was difficult: he thought he would return it to her, saying that it was beyond him. Just then she and his uncle entered: they were talking together, and did not perceive him.

'No, it's no use, Isabel,' said his uncle. 'He's got no curiosity, no leanings: it would only disgust him and put him off. That's not the way to win souls. Owen thinks so, too. And he's too innocent: why when I was his age . . . Why, there's Francis. What's the boy reading? Ah, I see! What do you make of it?'

Francis closed the book.

'I give it up,' he said. 'I can't get on with it.'

Mrs. Ray laughed.

'I agree, too, Horace,' she said. 'But what a pity!'

Somehow Francis got the impression, he remembered, that they had been talking about him. But, if so, *what* was it for which he had no leanings?'

He had gone to bed rather early that night, encouraged, he thought, to do so, leaving the rest at a game of Bridge. He soon slept, but awoke, thinking he heard the sound of chanting. Then came three strokes of a bell, and a pause and three more. He was too sleepy to care what it was about.

Such, as the train rushed through the night, was the sum of his impressions about his visit to the man whose substance he had now inherited, subject to the charge of £500 a year to the Reverend Owen Barton. He was astonished to find how vivid and how vaguely disquieting were these memories, which now for four years had been buried in his mind. As he sank into sounder sleep they faded again, and he thought little more of them in the morning.

He went to see Mr. Angus as soon as he got to London. Certain securities would have to be sold in order to pay death duties, but the administration of the estate was a simple matter. Francis wanted to know more about his benefactor, but Mr. Angus could tell him very little. Horace Elton had, for some years, lived an extremely sequestered life down at Wedderburn, and his only intimate associate was his secretary, this Mr. Owen Barton. Beyond him, there were two ladies who used often to stay with him for long periods. Their names?—and he paused, searching his memory.

'Mrs. Isabel Ray and her daughter Judith?' suggested Francis.

'Exactly. They were often there. And, not infrequently, a number of people used to arrive rather late in the evening, eleven o'clock or even later, stay for an hour or two and then be off again. A little mysterious. Only a week or so before Mr.

Elton died, there had been quite a congregation of them, fifteen or twenty, I believe.'

Francis was silent for a moment: it was as if pieces of jig-saw puzzle were calling for their due location. But their shapes were too fantastic. . . .

'And about my uncle's illness and death,' he said. 'The cremation of his body was on the same day as that on which he died; at least so I understood from your telegram.'

'Yes: that was so,' said Mr. Angus.

'But why? I should instantly have come back to England in order to be present. Was it not unusual?'

'Yes, Mr. Elton, it was unusual. But there were reasons for it.'

'I should like to hear them,' he said. 'I was his heir, and it would have been only proper that I should have been there. Why?'

Angus hesitated a moment.

'That is a reasonable question,' he said, 'and I feel bound to answer it. I must begin a little way back. . . . Your Uncle was in excellent physical health apparently, till about a week before his death. Very stout, but very alert and active. Then the trouble began. It took the form at first of some grievous mental and spiritual disturbance. He thought for some reason that he was going to die very soon, and the idea of death produced in him an abnormal panic terror. He telegraphed for me, for he wanted to make some alteration in his will. I was away and could not get down till the next day, and by the time I arrived he was too desperately ill to give any sort of coherent instructions. But his intention, I think, was to cut Mr. Owen Barton out of it.'

Again the lawyer paused.

'I found,' he said, 'that on the morning of the day I got down to Wedderburn, he had sent for the parson of his parish, and had made a confession to him. What that was I have not, of course, the slightest idea. Till then he had been in this panic fear of death, but was physically himself. Immediately afterwards some very horrible disease invaded him. Just that: invasion. The doctors who were summoned from London and Bournemouth had no idea what it was. Some unknown microbe, they supposed, which made the most swift and frightful havoc of skin and tissue and bone. It was like some putrefying internal corruption. It was as if he was dead already.... Really, I don't know what good it will do to tell you this.'

'I want to know,' said Francis.

'Well: this corruption. Living organisms came out as from a dead body. His nurses used to be sick. And the room was always swarming with flies; great fat flies, crawling over the walls and the bed. He was quite conscious, and there persisted this frantic terror of death, when you would have thought that a man's soul would have been only too thankful to be quit of such a habitation.'

'And was Mr. Owen Barton with him?' asked Francis.

'From the moment that Mr. Elton made his confession, he refused to see him. Once he came into the room, and there was a shocking scene. The dying man screamed and yelled with terror. Nor would he see the two ladies we have mentioned: why they continued to stop in the house I can't imagine. Then on the last morning of his life—he could not speak now—he traced a word or two on a piece of paper, and it seemed that he wanted to receive the Holy Communion. So the parson was sent for.'

The old lawyer paused again: Francis saw that his hand was shaking:

'Then very dreadful things happened,' he said. 'I was in the room, for he signed to me to be near him, and I saw them with my own eyes. The parson had poured the wine into the chalice, and had put the bread on the paten, and was about to consecrate the elements, when a cloud of those flies, of which I have told you, came about him. They filled the chalice like a swarm of bees, they settled in their unclean thousands on the paten, and in a couple of minutes the chalice was dry and empty and they had devoured the bread. Then like drilled hosts, you may say, they swarmed on to your uncle's face, so that you could see nothing of it. He choked and he gasped: there was one writhing convulsion, and, thank God, it was all over.'

'And then?' asked Francis.

'There were no flies. Nothing. But it was necessary to have the body cremated at once and the bedding with it. Very shocking indeed! I would not have told you, if you had not pressed me.'

'And the ashes?' asked he.

'You will see that there is a clause in his will, directing that his remains should be buried at the foot of the Judas-tree beside the swimming pool in the garden at Wedderburn. That was done.'

Francis was a very unimaginative young man, free from superstitious twitterings and unprofitable speculations, and this story, suggestive though it was, of ghastly sub-currents, did not take hold of his mind at all or lead to the fashioning of uneasy fancies. It was all very horrible, but it was over. He went down to Wedderburn for Easter with a widowed sister of his and her small boy, aged eleven, and they all fairly fell in love with the place. It was soon settled that Sybil Marsham should let her house in London for the summer months, and establish herself here. Dickie, who was a delicate boy, rather queer and elfin, would thus have the benefit of country air, and Francis the benefit of having the place run by his sister and occupied and in commission whenever he was able to get away from his work.

The house was of brick and timber, with accommodation for half a dozen folk, and stood on high ground above the little town. Francis made a tour of it, as soon as he arrived, rather astonished to find how the sight of it rubbed up to clearness in the minutest details his memory of it. There was the sitting-room with its tall bookcases and its deep window-seats overlooking the garden, where he had sat unobserved when his uncle and Mrs. Ray came in talking together. Above was his uncle's panelled bedroom, which he proposed to occupy himself, with the big wardrobe containing vestments. He opened it: they were under their covering sheets of tissue paper, shimmering with scarlet and gold and finest lawn foamed with Irish lace: a faint smell of incense hung about them. Next there was his uncle's sitting-room, and beyond that the room which he had slept in before, and was now appropriated to Dickie. These rooms lay on the front of the house, looking westwards over the garden, and he went out to renew acquaintance with it. Flower-beds gay with spring blossoms ran below the windows: then came the lawn, and beyond the belt of trees that enclosed the swimming pool. He passed along the path that threaded it between tapestries of primrose and anemone, and came out into the clearing that surrounded the water. The bathing shed stood at the deep end of it by the sluice that splashed riotously into the channel below, for the stream that supplied the pool was running full with the rains of March. In front of the copse on the far side stood a Judas-tree decked gloriously with flowers, and the reflection of it was cast waveringly on the rippled surface of the water. Somewhere below those red-blossoming boughs, there was buried a casket of ashes. He strolled round the pool: it was quite sheltered here from the April breeze, and bees were busy in the red blossoms. Bees, and large fat flies, a quantity of them.

He and Sybil were sitting in the drawing-room with the deep window-seats as dusk began to fall. A servant came in to say that Mr. Owen Barton had called. Certainly they were at home, and he entered, and was introduced to Sybil.

'You will hardly remember me, Mr. Elton,' he said, 'but I was here when you paid a visit to your uncle: four years ago it must have been.'

'But I remember you perfectly,' he said. 'We bathed together, we played tennis: you were very kind to a shy boy. And are you living here still?'

'Yes: I took a house in Wedderburn after your uncle's death. I spent six very happy years with him as his secretary, and I got much attached to the country. My house stands just outside your garden palings opposite the latched gate leading into the wood round the pool.'

The door opened and Dickie came in. He caught sight of the stranger and stopped.

'Say "how do you do" to Mr. Barton, Dickie,' said his mother.

Dickie performed this duty with due politeness and stood regarding him. He was a shy boy usually; but, after this inspection, he advanced close to him, and laid his hands on his knees.

'I like you,' he said confidently, and leant up against him.

'Don't bother Mr. Barton, Dickie,' she said rather sharply.

'But indeed he's doing nothing of the kind,' said Barton, and he drew the boy towards him so that he stood clipped between his knees.

Sybil got up.

'Come, Dick,' she said. 'We'll have a walk round the garden before it gets dark.'

'Is he coming, too?' asked the boy.

'No: he's going to stop and talk to Uncle Francis.'

When the two men were alone Barton said a word or two about Horace Elton, who had always been so generous a friend to him. The end, mercifully short, had been terrible, and terrible to him personally had been the dying man's refusal to see him during the last two days of his life.

'His mind, I think, must have been affected,' he said, 'by his awful sufferings. It happens like that sometimes: people turn against those with whom they have been most intimate. I have often mourned over that, and deeply regretted it. . . . And I owe you a certain word of explanation, Mr. Elton. No doubt you were puzzled to find in your uncle's will that I was entitled "the Reverend". It is quite true, though I do not call myself so. Certain spiritual doubts and difficulties caused me to give up my orders, but your uncle always held that if a man is once a priest he is always a priest. He was very strong about that, and no doubt he was right.'

'I didn't know my uncle took any interest in ecclesiastical

affairs,' said Francis. 'Ah, I had forgotten about his vestments. Perhaps that was only an artistic taste.'

'By no means. He regarded them as sacred things, consecrated to holy uses. . . . And may I ask you what happened to his remains? I remember he once expressed a wish to be buried by the swimming pool.'

'His body was cremated,' said Francis, 'and the ashes were buried there.'

Barton stayed but little longer, and Sybil on her return was frankly relieved to find he had gone. Simply, she didn't like him. There was something queer, something sinister about him. Francis laughed at her: quite a good fellow, he thought.

Dreams, of course, are a mere hash-up of recent mental images and associations, and a very vivid dream that came to Francis that night could easily have arisen from such topics. He thought he was swimming in the bathing pool with Owen Barton, and that his uncle, stout and florid, was standing underneath the Judas-tree watching them. That seemed quite natural, as is the way of dreams: merely he was not dead at all. When they came out of the water, he looked for his clothes, but found that there was laid out for him a scarlet cassock and a white lace-trimmed cotta. This again was quite natural; so, too, was the fact that Barton put on a gold cope.

His uncle, very merry and licking his lips, joined them, and each of them took an arm of his and they walked back to the house together singing a hymn. As they went the daylight died, and by the time they crossed the lawn it was black night, and the windows of the house were lit. They walked upstairs, still singing, into his uncle's bedroom which was now his own. There was an open door, which he had never noticed before opposite his bed, and there came a very bright light from it. Then the sense of nightmare began, for his two companions, gripping him tightly, pulled him along towards it, and he struggled with them knowing there was something terrible within. But step by step they dragged him, violently resisting, and now out of the door there came a swarm of large fat flies that buzzed and settled on him. Thicker and thicker they streamed out, covering his face, and crawling into his eyes, and entering his mouth as he panted for breath. The horror grew to breaking-point, and he woke sweating with a hammering heart. He switched on the light, and there was the quiet room and the dawn beginning to be luminous outside, and the birds just tuning up.

Francis's few days of holiday passed quickly. He went down to the village to see Barton's house, and found it a most pleasant little dwelling, and its owner an exceedingly pleasant fellow. Barton dined with them one evening, and Sybil went so far as to admit that her first judgment of him was hasty. He was charming with Dickie, too, and that disposed her in his favour, and the boy adored him. Soon it was necessary to find some tutor for him, and Barton readily agreed to undertake his education, and every morning Dickie trotted across the garden and through the wood where the swimming pool lay to Barton's house. His ill-health had made him rather backward in his studies, but he was now eager to learn and to please his instructor, and he got on quickly.

* * *

It was now that I first met Francis, and during the next few months in London we became close friends. He told me that he had lately inherited this place at Wedderburn from his uncle, but for the present I knew no more than that of the previous history which I have just recorded. Sometime during July he told me he was intending to spend the month of August there. His sister, who kept house for him, and her small boy would be away for the first week or two, for she had taken him off to the seaside. Would I then come and share his solitude, and get on there, uninterrupted, with some work I had on hand. That seemed a very attractive plan, and we motored down together one very hot afternoon early in August, that promised thunder. Owen Barton, he told me, who had been his uncle's secretary, was coming to dine with us that night.

It wanted an hour or so yet to dinner-time when we arrived, and Francis directed me, if I cared for a dip, to the bathing pool among the trees beyond the lawn. He had various household businesses to look into himself, so I went off alone. It was an enchanting place, the water still and very clear, mirroring the sky and the full-foliaged trees, and I stripped and plunged in. I lay and floated in the cool water, I swam and dived again, and then I saw, walking close to the far bank of the pool, a man of something more than middle-age, and extremely stout. He was in dress clothes, dinner-jacket and black tie, and instantly it struck me that this must be Mr. Barton coming up from the village to dine with us. It must therefore be later than I thought, and I swam back to the shed where my clothes were. As I climbed out of the water, I glanced round. There was no one there.

It was a slight shock, but very slight. It was odd that he should have come so unexpectedly out of the wood and disappeared again so suddenly, but it did not concern me much. I hurried home, changed quickly and came down, expecting to find Francis and his guest in the drawing-room. But I need not have been in such haste for now my watch told me that there was still a quarter of an hour before dinner-time. As for the others, I supposed that Mr. Barton was upstairs with Francis in his sitting-room. So I picked up a chance book to beguile the time, and read for a while, but the room grew rather dark, and, rising to switch on the electric light, I saw standing outside the french window into the garden the figure of a man, outlined against the last of a stormy sunset, looking into the room.

There was no doubt whatever in my mind that he was the same person as I had seen when I was bathing, and the switching on of the light made this clear, for it shone full on his face. No doubt then Mr. Barton finding he was too early was strolling about the garden till the dinner-hour. But now I did not look forward at all to this evening: I had had a good look at him and there was something horrible about him. Was he human, was he earthly at all? Then he quietly moved away, and immediately afterwards there came a knock at the front door just outside the room, and I heard Francis coming downstairs. Hc went to the door himself: there was a word of greeting, and he came into the room accompanied by a tall, slim fellow whom he introduced to me.

We had a very pleasant evening: Barton talked fluently and agreeably, and more than once he spoke of his friend and pupil Dickie. About eleven he rose to go, and Francis suggested to him that he should walk back across the garden which gave him a short cut to his house. The threatening storm still held off, but it was very dark overhead, as we stood together outside the french window. Barton was soon swallowed up in the blackness. Then there came a bright flash of lightning, and in that moment of illumination I saw that there was standing in the middle of the lawn, as if waiting for him, the figure I had seen twice already. 'Who is that?' was on the tip of my tongue, but instantly I perceived that Francis had seen nothing of it, and so I was silent, for I knew now what I had already half-guessed that this was no living man of flesh and blood whom I had seen. A few heavy drops of rain plopped on the flagged walk, and, as we moved indoors, Francis called out, 'Good night, Barton!' and the cheery voice answered.

Before long we went up to bed, and he took me into his room as we passed, a big panelled chamber with a great wardrobe by the bed. Close to it hung an oil-portrait of kit-cat size.

'I'll show you what's in that wardrobe tomorrow,' he said. 'Rather wonderful things. . . . That's a picture of my uncle.'

I had seen that face before this evening.

For the next two or three days I had no further glimpse of that dreadful visitant, but never for a moment was I at ease, for I was aware that he was about. What instinct or what sense perceived that, I have no idea: perhaps it was merely the dread I had of seeing him again that gave rise to the conviction. I thought of telling Francis that I must get back to London;

what prevented me from so doing was the desire to know more, and that made me fight this cold fear. Then very soon I perceived that Francis was no more at ease than I was. Sometimes as we sat together in the evening he was oddly alert: he would pause in the middle of a sentence as if some sound had attracted his attention, or he would look up from our game of bezique and focus his eyes for a second on some corner of the room or, more often, on the dark oblong of the open french window. Had he, I wondered, been seeing something invisible to me, and, like myself, feared to speak of it?

These impressions were momentary and infrequent, but they kept alive in me the feeling that there was something astir, and that something, coming out of the dark and the unknown, was growing in force. It had come into the house, and was present everywhere.... And then one awoke again to a morning of heavenly brightness and sunshine, and surely one was disquieting oneself in vain.

I had been there about a week when something occurred which precipitated what followed. I slept in the room which Dickie usually occupied, and awoke one night feeling uncomfortably hot. I tugged at a blanket to remove it, but it was tucked very tightly in between the mattresses on the side of the bed next to the wall. Eventually I got it free, and as I did so I heard something drop with a flutter on to the floor. In the morning I remembered that, and found underneath the bed a little paper notebook. I opened it idly enough, and within were a dozen pages written over in a round childish handwriting, and these words struck my eye:

'Thursday, July 11th. I saw great-uncle Horace again this morning in the wood. He told me something about myself which I didn't understand, but he said I should like it when I got older. I mustn't tell anybody that he's here, nor what he told me, except Mr. Barton.'

I did not care one jot whether I was reading a boy's private diary. That was no longer a consideration worth thinking about. I turned over the page and found another entry.

'Sunday, July 21st. I saw Uncle Horace again. I said I had told Mr. Barton what he had told me, and Mr. Barton had told me some more things, and that he was pleased, and said I was getting on and that he would take me to prayers some day soon.'

I cannot describe the thrill of horror that these entries woke in me. They made the apparition which I had seen infinitely more real and more sinister. It was a spirit corrupt and malign and intent on corruption that haunted the place. But what was I to do? How could I, without any lead from Francis, tell him that the spirit of his uncle—of whom at present I knew nothing—had been seen not by me only, but by his nephew, and that he was at work on the boy's mind? Then there was the mention of Barton. Certainly that could not be left as it was. He was collaborating in that damnable task. A cult of corruption (or was I being too fantastic?) began to outline itself. Then what did that sentence about taking him to prayers mean? But Dickie was away, thank goodness, for the present, and there was time to think it over. As for that pitiful little notebook, I put it into a locked despatch case.

The day, as far as outward and visible signs were concerned, passed pleasantly. For me there was a morning's work, and for both of us an afternoon on the golf-links. But below there was something heavy; my knowledge of that diary kept intervening with mental telephone-calls asking 'What are you going to *do*?' Francis, on his side, was troubled; there were sub-currents, and I did not know what they were. Silences fell, not the natural unobserved silences between those who are intimate, which are only a symbol of their intimacy, but the silences between those who have something on their minds of which they fear to speak. These had got more stringent all day: there was a growing tenseness: all common topics were banal, for they only cloaked a certain topic.

We sat out on the lawn before dinner on that sultry evening, and breaking one of these silent intervals, he pointed at the front of the house.

'There's an odd thing,' he said. 'Look! There are three rooms aren't there on the ground floor: dining-room, drawing-room, and the little study where you write. Now look above. There are three rooms there: your bedroom, my bedroom, and my sitting-room. I've measured them. There are twelve feet missing. Looks as if there was a sealed-up room somewhere.'

Here, at any rate, was something to talk about.

'Exciting,' I said. 'Mayn't we explore?'

'We will. We'll explore as soon as we've dined. Then there's another thing: quite off the point. You remember those vestments I showed you the other day? I opened the wardrobe, where they are kept, an hour ago, and a lot of big fat flies came buzzing out. A row like a dozen aeroplanes overhead. Remote but loud, if you know what I mean. And then there weren't any.'

Somehow I felt that what we had been silent about was coming out into the open. It might be ill to look upon. . . .

He jumped from his chair.

'Let's have done with these silences,' he cried. 'He's here, my uncle, I mean. I haven't told you yet, but he died in a swarm of flies. He asked for the Sacrament, but before the wine was consecrated the chalice was choked with them. And I know he's here. It sounds damned rot, but he is.'

'I know that, too,' I said. 'I've seen him.'

'Why didn't you tell me?'

'Because I thought you would laugh at me.'

'I should have a few days ago,' said he. 'But I don't now. Go on.'

'The first evening I was here I saw him at the bathing pool. That same night, when we were seeing Owen Barton off, a flash of lightning came, and he was there again standing on the lawn.'

'But how did you know it was he?' asked Francis.

'I knew it when you showed me the portrait of him in your bedroom that same night. Have you seen him?'

'No; but he's here. Anything more?'

This was the opportunity not only natural but inevitable.

'Yes, much more,' I said. 'Dickie has seen him too.'

'That child? Impossible.'

The door out of the drawing-room opened, and Francis's parlour-maid came out with the sherry on a tray. She put the decanter and glasses down on the wicker table between us, and I asked her to bring out the despatch case from my room. I took the paper notebook out of it.

'This slipped out from between my mattresses last night. It's Dickie's diary. Listen': and I read him the first extract.

Francis gave one of those swift disconcerting glances over his shoulder.

'But we're dreaming,' he said. 'It's a nightmare. God, there's something awful here! And what about Dickie not telling anybody except Barton what he told him? Anything more?'

'Yes. "Sunday, July 21st. I saw Uncle Horace again. I said I had told Mr. Barton what he told me, and Mr. Barton told me some more things, and that he was pleased and said I was getting on, and that he would take me to prayers some day soon. I don't know what that means." '

Francis sprang out of his chair.

'What?' he cried. 'Take him to prayers? Wait a minute. Let me remember about my first visit here. I was a boy of nineteen, and frightfully, absurdly innocent for my age. A woman staying here gave me a book to read called *Là-Bas*. I didn't get far in it then, but I know what it's about now.'

'Black Mass,' said I. 'Satan worshippers.'

'Yes. Then one day my uncle dressed me up in a scarlet cassock, and Barton came in and put on a cope and said something about my being a server. He used to be a priest, did you know that? And one night I awoke and heard the sound of chanting and a bell rang. By the way, Barton's coming to dine tomorrow. . . .'

'What are you going to do?'

'About him? I can't tell yet. But we've got something to do tonight. Horrors have happened here in this house. There must be some room where they held their Mass, a chapel. Why, there's that missing space I spoke of just now.'

After dinner we set to work. Somewhere on the first floor on the garden front of the house there was this space unaccounted for by the dimensions of the rooms there. We turned on the electric light in all of them, and then going out into the garden we saw that the windows in Francis's bedroom and in his sitting-room next door were far more widely spaced than they should have been. Somewhere, then, between them lay the area to which there was no apparent access and we went upstairs. The wall of his sitting-room seemed solid, it was of brick and timber, and large beams ran through it at narrow intervals. But the wall of his bedroom was panelled, and when we tapped on it, no sound came through into the other room beyond.

We began to examine it.

The servants had gone to bed, and the house was silent, but as we moved about from garden to house and from one room to another there was some presence watching and following us. We had shut the door into his bedroom from the passage, but now as we peered and felt about the panelling, the door swung open and closed again, and something entered, brushing my shoulder as it passed.

'What's that?' I said. 'Someone came in.'

'Never mind that,' he said. 'Look what I've found.'

In the border of one of the panels was a black stud like an ebony bell-push. He pressed it and pulled, and a section of the panelling slid sideways, disclosing a red curtain cloaking a doorway. He drew it aside with a clash of metal rings. It was dark within, and out of the darkness came a smell of stale incense. I felt with my hand along the frame of the doorway and found a switch, and the blackness was flooded with a dazzling light.

Within was a chapel. There was no window, and at the West end of it (not the East) there stood an altar. Above it was a picture, evidently of some early Italian school. It was on the lines of the Fra Angelico picture of the Annunciation. The Virgin sat in an open loggia, and on the flowery space outside the angel made his salutation. His spreading wings were the wings of a bat, and his black head and neck were those of a raven. He had his left hand, not his right, raised in blessing. The virgin's robe of thinnest red muslin was trimmed with revolting symbols, and her face was that of a panting dog with tongue protruding.

There were two niches at the East end, in which were marble statues of naked men, with the inscriptions 'St. Judas' and 'St. Gilles de Raies'. One was picking up pieces of silver that lay at his feet, the other looked down leering and laughing at the prone figure of a mutilated boy. The place was lit by a chandelier from the ceiling: this was of the shape of a crown of thorns and electric bulbs nestled among the woven silver twigs. A bell hung from the roof, close beside the altar.

For the moment, as I looked on these obscene blasphemies, I felt that they were merely grotesque and no more to be regarded seriously than the dirty inscriptions written upon empty wall-spaces in the street. That indifference swiftly passed, and a horrified consciousness of the devotion of those who had fashioned and assembled these decorations took its place. Skilled painters and artificers had wrought them and they were here for the service of all that is evil; that spirit of adoration lived in them dynamic and active. And the place was throbbing with the exultant joy of those who had worshipped here.

'And look here!' called Francis. He pointed to a little table standing against the wall just outside the altar-rails.

There were photographs on it, one of a boy standing on the header-board at the bathing pool about to plunge.

'That's me,' he said. 'Barton took it. And what's written underneath it? "Ora pro Francisco Elton." And that's Mrs. Ray, and that's my uncle, and that's Barton in a cope. Pray for him, too, please. But it's childish!'

He suddenly burst into a shout of laughter. The roof of the chapel was vaulted and the echo that came from it was loud and surprising, the place rang with it. His laughter ceased, but not so the echo. There was someone else laughing. But where?

Who? Except for us the chapel was empty of all visible presences.

On and on the laughter went, and we stared at each other with panic stirring. The brilliant light from the chandelier began to fade, dusk gathered, and in the dusk there was brewing some hellish and deadly force. And through the dimness I saw, hanging in the air, and oscillating slightly as if in a draught the laughing face of Horace Elton. Francis saw it too.

'Fight it! Withstand it!' he cried as he pointed to it. 'Desecrate all that it holds sanctified! God, do you smell the incense and the corruption?'

We tore the photographs, we smashed the table on which they stood. We plucked the frontal from the altar and spat on the accursed table: we tugged at it till it toppled over and the marble slab split in half. We hauled from the niches the two statues that stood there, and crash they went on to the paved floor. Then appalled at the riot of our iconoclasm we paused. The laughter had ceased and no oscillating face dangled in the dimness. Then we left the chapel and pulled across the doorway the panel that closed it.

Francis came to sleep in my room, and we talked long, laying our plans for next day. We had forgotten the picture over the altar in our destruction, but now it worked in with what we proposed to do. Then we slept, and the night passed without disturbance. At the least we had broken up the apparatus that was hallowed to unhallowed uses, and that was something. But there was grim work ahead yet, and the issue was unconjecturable.

Barton came to dine that next evening, and there hung on the wall opposite his place the picture from the chapel upstairs. He did not notice it at first, for the room was rather dark, but not dark enough yet to need artificial light. He was gay and lively as usual, spoke amusingly and wittily, and asked when his friend Dickie was to return. Towards the end of dinner the lights were switched on, and then he saw the picture. I was watching him, and the sweat started out on his face that had grown clay-coloured in a moment. Then he pulled himself together.

'That's a strange picture,' he said. 'Was it here before? Surely not.'

'No: it was in a room upstairs,' said Francis. 'About Dickie? I don't know for certain when he'll come back. We have found his diary, and presently we must speak about that.'

'Dickie's diary? Indeed!' said Barton, and he moistened his lips with his tongue.

I think he guessed then that there was something desperate ahead, and I pictured a man condemned to be hanged waiting in his cell with his warders for the imminent hour, as Barton waited then. He sat with an elbow on the table and his hand propping his forehead. Immediately almost the servant brought in our coffee and left us.

'Dickie's diary,' said Francis quietly. 'Your name figures in it. Also my uncle's. Dickie saw him more than once. But, of course, you know that.'

Barton drank off his glass of brandy.

'Are you telling me a ghost story?' he said. 'Pray go on.'

'Yes, it's partly a ghost story, but not entirely. My uncle—his ghost if you like—told him certain stories and said he must keep them secret except from you. And you told him more. And you said he should come to prayers with you some day soon. Where was that to be? In the room just above us?'

The brandy had given the condemned man a momentary courage.

'A pack of lies, Mr. Elton,' he said. 'That boy has got a corrupt mind. He told me things that no boy of his age should know: he giggled and laughed at them. Perhaps I ought to have told his mother.'

'It's too late to think of that now,' said Francis. 'The diary I spoke of will be in the hands of the police at ten o'clock to-morrow morning. They will also inspect the room upstairs where you have been in the habit of celebrating the Black Mass.'

Barton leant forward towards him.

'No, no,' he cried. 'Don't do that! I beg and implore you! I will confess the truth to you. I will conceal nothing. My life has been a blasphemy. But I'm sorry: I repent. I abjure all those abominations from henceforth: I renounce them all in the name of Almighty God.'

'Too late,' said Francis.

And then the horror that haunts me still began to manifest itself. The wretched man threw himself back in his chair, and there dropped from his forehead on to his white shirt-front a long grey worm that lay and wriggled there. At that moment there came from overhead the sound of a bell, and he sprang to his feet.

'No!' he cried again. 'I retract all I said. I abjure nothing. And my Lord is waiting for me in the sanctuary. I must be quick and make my humble confession to him.'

With the movement of a slinking animal he slid from the room, and we heard his steps going swiftly upstairs.

'Did you see?' I whispered. 'And what's to be done? Is the man sane?'

'It's beyond us now,' said Francis.

There was a thump on the ceiling overhead as if someone had fallen, and without a word we ran upstairs into Francis's bedroom. The door of the wardrobe where the vestments were kept was open, some lay on the floor. The panel was open, too, but within it was dark. In terror at what might meet our eyes, I felt for the switch and turned the light on.

The bell which had sounded a few minutes ago was still swinging gently, though speaking no more. Barton, clad in the gold-embroidered cope, lay in front of the overturned altar, with his face twitching. Then that ceased, the rattle of death creaked in his throat, and his mouth fell open. Great flies, swarms of them, coming from nowhere, settled on it.

One of the most famous of all writers of horror stories was *Algernon Blackwood*—the world traveller, journalist, farmer, hotelier and one-time gold prospector who packed a wealth of personal experience into all his stories. His work bears the stamp of authenticity and in few items is this more obvious than 'Ancient Sorceries'. It is told in Blackwood's deceptively lazy style, jogging the reader quietly into a situation of mounting terror. How deep Blackwood's knowledge of Satanism went it is difficult to judge in hindsight, but he did write about devil worship and witchcraft in a number of other short stories and all have a convincing ring about them. Featured in this story is one of the author's most fascinating creations, Dr. Silence, an investigator of the occult who helps unravel the terrible puzzle of a man who believes he is trapped in a village totally occupied by Satanists. . . .

Ancient Sorceries

ALGERNON BLACKWOOD

There are, it would appear, certain wholly unremarkable persons, with none of the characteristics that invite adventure, who yet once or twice in the course of their smooth lives undergo an experience so strange that the world catches its breath—and looks the other way! And it was cases of this kind, perhaps, more than any other, that fell into the widespread net of John Silence, the psychic doctor, and, appealing to his deep humanity, to his patience, and to his great qualities of spiritual sympathy, led often to the revelation of problems of the strangest complexity, and of the profoundest possible human interest.

Matters that seemed almost too curious and fantastic for belief he loved to trace to their hidden sources. To unravel a tangle in the very soul of things—and to release a suffering human soul in the process—was with him a veritable passion. And the knots he untied were, indeed, often passing strange.

The world, of course, asks for some plausible basis to which it can attach credence—something it can, at last, pretend to explain. The adventurous type it can understand: such people carry about with them an adequate explanation of their exciting lives, and their characters obviously drive them into the circumstances which produce the adventures. It expects nothing else from them, and is satisfied. But dull, ordinary folk have no right to out-of-the-way experiences, and the world having been led to expect otherwise, is disappointed with them, not to say shocked. Its complacent judgment has been rudely disturbed.

'Such a thing happen to *that* man!' it cries—'a commonplace person like that! It is too absurd! There must be something wrong!'

Yet there could be no question that something did actually happen to little Arthur Vezin, something of the curious nature he described to Dr. Silence. Outwardly, or inwardly, it happened beyond a doubt, and in spite of the jeers of his few friends who heard the tale, and observed wisely that 'such a thing might perhaps have come to Iszard, that crack-brained Iszard, or to that odd fish Minski, but it could never have happened to commonplace little Vezin, who was fore-ordained to live and die according to scale.'

But, whatever his method of death was, Vezin certainly did not 'live according to scale' so far as this particular event in his otherwise uneventful life was concerned; and to hear him recount it, and watch his pale delicate features change, and hear his voice grow softer and more hushed as he proceeded, was to know the conviction that his halting words perhaps failed sometimes to convey. He lived the thing over again each time he told it. His whole personality became muffled in the recital. It subdued him more than ever, so that the tale became a lengthy apology for an experience that he deprecated. He appeared to excuse himself and ask your pardon for having dared to take part in so fantastic an episode. For little Vezin was a timid, gentle, sensitive soul, rarely able to assert himself, tender to man and beast, and almost constitutionally unable to say No, or to claim many things that should rightly have been his. His whole scheme of life seemed utterly remote from anything more exciting than missing a train or losing an umbrella on an omnibus. And when this curious event came upon him he was already more years beyond forty than his friends suspected or he cared to admit.

John Silence, who heard him speak of his experience more than once, said that he sometimes left out certain details and put in others; yet they were all obviously true. The whole scene was unforgettably cinematographed on to his mind. None of the details were imagined or invented. And when he told the story with them all complete, the effect was undeniable. His appealing brown eyes shone, and much of the charming personality, usually so carefully repressed, came forward and revealed itself. His modesty was always there, of course, but in the telling he forgot the present and allowed himself to appear almost vividly as he lived again in the past of his adventure.

He was on the way home when it happened, crossing northern France from some mountain trip or other where he buried himself solitary-wise every summer. He had nothing but an unregistered bag in the rack, and the train was jammed to suffocation, most of the passengers being unredeemed holiday English. He disliked them, not because they were his fellow-countrymen, but because they were noisy and obtrusive, obliterating with their big limbs and tweed clothing all the quieter tints of the day that brought him satisfaction and enabled him to melt into insignificance and forget that he was anybody. These English clashed about him like a brass band, making him feel vaguely that he ought to be more self-assertive and obstreperous, and that he did not claim insistently enough all kinds of things that he didn't want and that were really valueless, such as corner seats, windows up or down, and so forth.

So that he felt uncomfortable in the train, and wished the journey were over and he was back again living with his unmarried sister in Surbiton.

And when the train stopped for ten panting minutes at the little station in northern France, and he got out to stretch his legs on the platform, and saw to his dismay a further batch of the British Isles debouching from another train, it suddenly seemed impossible to him to continue the journey. Even *his* flabby soul revolted, and the idea of staying a night in the little town and going on next day by a slower, emptier train, flashed into his mind. The guard was already shouting '*en voiture*' and the corridor of his compartment was already packed when the thought came to him. And, for once, he acted with decision and rushed to snatch his bag.

Finding the corridor and steps impassable, he tapped at the window (for he had a corner seat) and begged the Frenchman who sat opposite to hand his luggage out to him, explaining in his wretched French that he intended to break the journey there. And this elderly Frenchman, he declared, gave him a look, half of warning, half of reproach, that to his dying day he could never forget; handed the bag through the window of the moving train; and at the same time poured into his ears a long sentence, spoken rapidly and low, of which he was able to comprehend only the last few words: '*à cause du sommeil et à cause des chats.*'

In reply to Dr. Silence, whose singular psychic acuteness at once seized upon this Frenchman as a vital point in the adventure, Vezin admitted that the man had impressed him favourably from the beginning, though without being able to explain why. They had sat facing one another during the four hours of the journey, and though no conversation had passed between them—Vezin was timid about his stuttering French—he confessed that his eyes were being continually drawn to his face, almost, he felt, to rudeness, and that each, by a dozen nameless little politenesses and attentions, had evinced the desire to be kind. The men liked each other and their personalities did not clash, or would not have clashed had they chanced to come to terms of acquaintance. The Frenchman, indeed, seemed to have exercised a silent protective influence over the insignificant little Englishman, and without words or gestures betrayed that he wished him well and would gladly have been of service to him.

'And this sentence that he hurled at you after the bag?' asked John Silence, smiling that peculiarly sympathetic smile that always melted the prejudices of his patient, 'were you unable to follow it exactly?'

'It was so quick and low and vehement,' explained Vezin, in his small voice, 'that I missed practically the whole of it. I only caught the few words at the very end, because he spoke them so clearly, and his face was bent down out of the carriage window so near to mine.'

'"*A cause du sommeil et à cause des chats*"?' repeated Dr. Silence, as though half speaking to himself.

'That's it exactly,' said Vezin; 'which, I take it, means something like "because of sleep and because of the cats," doesn't it?'

'Certainly, that's how I should translate it,' the doctor observed shortly, evidently not wishing to interrupt more than necessary.

'And the rest of the sentence—all the first part I couldn't understand, I mean—was a warning not to do something—not to stop in the town, or at some particular place in the town, perhaps. That was the impression it made on me.'

Then, of course, the train rushed off, and left Vezin standing on the platform alone and rather forlorn.

The little town climbed in straggling fashion up a sharp hill rising out of the plain at the back of the station, and was crowned by the twin towers of the ruined cathedral peeping over the summit. From the station itself it looked uninteresting and modern, but the fact was that the mediæval position lay out of sight just beyond the crest. And once he reached the top and entered the old streets, he stepped clean out of modern life into a bygone century. The noise and bustle of the crowded trained seemed days away. The spirit of this silent hill-town, remote from tourists and motor-cars, dreaming its own quiet life under the autumn sun, rose up and cast its spell upon him. Long before he recognised this spell he acted under it. He walked softly, almost on tiptoe, down the winding narrow streets where the gables all but met over his head, and he entered the doorway of the solitary inn with a deprecating and modest demeanour that was in itself an apology for intruding upon the place and disturbing its dream.

At first, however, Vezin said, he noticed very little of all this. The attempt at analysis came much later. What struck him then was only the delightful contrast of the silence and peace after the dust and noisy rattle of the train. He felt soothed and stroked like a cat.

'Like a cat, you said?' interrupted John Silence, quickly catching him up.

'Yes. At the very start I felt that.' He laughed apologetically. 'I felt as though the warmth and the stillness and the comfort made me purr. It seemed to be the general mood of the whole place—then.'

The inn, a rambling ancient house, the atmosphere of the old coaching days still about it, apparently did not welcome him too warmly. He felt he was only tolerated, he said. But it was cheap and comfortable, and the delicious cup of afternoon tea he ordered at once made him feel really very pleased with himself for leaving the train in this bold, original way. For to him it had seemed bold and original. He felt something of a dog. His room, too, soothed him with its dark panelling and low irregular ceiling, and the long sloping passage that led to it seemed the natural pathway to a real Chamber of Sleep—a little dim cubby hole out of the world where noise could not enter. It looked upon the courtyard at the back. It was all very charming, and made him think of himself as dressed in very soft velvet somehow, and the floors seemed padded, the walls provided with cushions. The sounds of the streets could not penetrate there. It was an atmosphere of absolute rest that surrounded him.

On engaging the two-franc room he had interviewed the only person who seemed to be about that sleepy afternoon, an elderly waiter with Dundreary whiskers and a drowsy courtesy, who had ambled lazily towards him across the stone yard; but on coming downstairs again for a little promenade in the town before dinner he encountered the proprietress herself. She was a large woman whose hands, feet, and features seemed to swim towards him out of a sea of person. They emerged, so to speak. But she had great dark, vivacious eyes that counteracted the bulk of her body, and betrayed the fact that in reality she was both vigorous and alert. When he first caught sight of her she was knitting in a low chair against the sunlight of the wall, and something at once made him see her as a great tabby cat, dozing, yet awake, heavily sleepy, and yet at the same time prepared for instantaneous action. A great mouser on the watch occurred to him.

She took him in with a single comprehensive glance that was polite without being cordial. Her neck, he noticed, was extraordinarily supple in spite of its proportions, for it turned so easily to follow him, and the head it carried bowed so very flexibly.

'But when she looked at me, you know,' said Vezin, with that little apologetic smile in his brown eyes, and that faintly deprecating gesture of the shoulders that was characteristic of him, 'the odd notion came to me that really she had intended to make quite a different movement, and that with a single bound she could have leaped at me across the width of that stone yard and pounced upon me like some huge cat upon a mouse.'

He laughed a little soft laugh, and Dr. Silence made a note in his book without interrupting, while Vezin proceeded in a tone as though he feared he had already told too much and more than we could believe.

'Very soft, yet very active she was, for all her size and mass, and I felt she knew what I was doing even after I had passed and was behind her back. She spoke to me, and her voice was smooth and running. She asked if I had my luggage, and was comfortable in my room, and then added that dinner was at seven o'clock, and that they were very early people in this little country town. Clearly, she intended to convey that late hours were not encouraged.'

Evidently, she contrived by voice and manner to give him the impression that here he would be 'managed', that everything would be arranged and planned for him, and that he had nothing to do but fall into the groove and obey. No decided action or sharp personal effort would be looked for from him. It was the very reverse of the train. He walked quietly out into the street feeling soothed and peaceful. He realised that he was in a *milieu* that suited him and stroked him the right way. It was so much easier to be obedient. He began to purr again, and to feel that all the town purred with him.

About the streets of that little town he meandered gently, falling deeper and deeper into the spirit of repose that characterised it. With no special aim he wandered up and down, and to and fro. The September sunshine fell slantingly over the roofs. Down winding alleyways, fringed with tumbling gables and open casements, he caught fairylike glimpses of the great plain below, and of the meadows and yellow copses lying like a dream-map in the haze. The spell of the past held very potently here, he felt.

The streets were full of picturesquely garbed men and women, all busy enough, going their respective ways; but no one took any notice of him or turned to stare at his obviously English appearance. He was even able to forget that with his tourist appearance he was a false note in a charming picture, and he melted more and more into the scene, feeling delightfully insignificant and unimportant and unselfconscious. It was like becoming part of a softly-coloured dream which he did not even realise to be a dream.

On the eastern side the hill fell away more sharply, and the plain below ran off rather suddenly into a sea of gathering shadows in which the little patches of woodland looked like islands and the stubble fields like deep water. Here he strolled along the old ramparts of ancient fortifications that once had been formidable, but now were only vision-like with their charming mingling of broken grey walls and wayward vine and ivy. From the broad coping on which he sat for a moment, level with the rounded tops of clipped plane trees, he saw the esplanade far below lying in shadow. Here and there a yellow sunbeam crept in and lay upon the fallen yellow leaves, and from the height he looked down and saw that the townsfolk were walking to and fro in the cool of the evening. He could just hear the sound of their slow footfalls, and the murmur of their voices floated up to him through the gaps between the trees. The figures looked like shadows as he caught glimpses of their quiet movements far below.

He sat there for some time pondering, bathed in the waves of murmurs and half-lost echoes that rose to his ears, muffled by the leaves of the plane trees. The whole town, and the little hill out of which it grew as naturally as an ancient wood, seemed to him like a being lying there half asleep on the plain and crooning to itself as it dozed.

And, presently, as he sat lazily melting into its dream, a sound of horns and strings and wood instruments rose to his ears, and the town band began to play at the far end of the crowded terrace below to the accompaniment of a very soft, deep-throated drum. Vezin was very sensitive to music, knew about it intelligently, and had even ventured, unknown to his friends, upon the composition of quiet melodies with low-running chords which he played to himself with the soft pedal when no one was about. And this music floating up through the trees from an invisible and doubtless very picturesque band of the townspeople wholly charmed him. He recognised nothing that they played, and it sounded as though they were simply improvising without a conductor. No definitely marked time ran through the pieces, which ended and began oddly after the fashion of wind through an Æolian harp. It was part of the place and scene, just as the dying sunlight and faintly-breathing wind were part of the scene and hour, and the mellow notes of old-fashioned plaintive horns, pierced here and there by the sharper strings, all half smothered by the continuous booming of the deep drum, touched his soul with a curiously potent spell that was almost too engrossing to be quite pleasant.

There was a certain queer sense of bewitchment in it all. The music seemed to him oddly unartificial. It made him think of trees swept by the wind, of night breezes singing among wires and chimney-stacks, or in the rigging of invisible ships; or—and the simile leaped up in his thoughts with a sudden sharpness of suggestion—a chorus of animals, of wild creatures, somewhere in desolate places of the world, crying and singing as animals will, to the moon. He could fancy he heard the wailing, half-human cries of cats upon the tiles at night, rising and falling with weird intervals of sound, and this music, muffled by distance and the trees, made him think of a queer company of these creatures on some roof far away in the sky, uttering their solemn music to one another and the moon in chorus.

It was, he felt at the time, a singular image to occur to him, yet it expressed his sensation pictorially better than anything else. The instruments played such impossibly odd intervals, and the crescendos and diminuendos were so very suggestive of cat-land on the tiles at night, rising swiftly, dropping without warning to deep notes again, and all in such strange confusion of discords and accords. But, at the same time a plaintive sweetness resulted on the whole, and the discords of these half-broken instruments were so singular that they did not distress his musical soul like fiddles out of tune.

He listened a long time, wholly surrendering himself as his character was, and then strolled homewards in the dusk as the air grew chilly.

'There was nothing to alarm?' put in Dr. Silence briefly.

'Absolutely nothing,' said Vezin; 'but you know it was all so fantastical and charming that my imagination was profoundly impressed. Perhaps, too,' he continued, gently explanatory, 'it was this stirring of my imagination that caused other impressions; for, as I walked back, the spell of the place began to steal over me in a dozen ways, though all intelligible ways. But there were other things I could not account for in the least, even then.'

'Incidents, you mean?'

'Hardly incidents, I think. A lot of vivid sensations crowded themselves upon my mind and I could trace them to no causes. It was just after sunset and the tumbled old buildings traced magical outlines against an opalescent sky of gold and red. The dusk was running down the twisted streets. All round the hill the plain pressed in like a dim sea, its level rising with the darkness. The spell of this kind of scene, you know, can be very moving, and it was so that night. Yet I felt that what came to me had nothing directly to do with the mystery and wonder of the scene.'

'Not merely the subtle transformations of the spirit that come with beauty,' put in the doctor, noticing his hesitation.

'Exactly,' Vezin went on, duly encouraged and no longer so fearful of our smiles at his expense. 'The impressions came from somewhere else. For instance, down the busy main street where men and women were bustling home from work, shopping at stalls and barrows, idly gossiping in groups, and all the rest of it, I saw that I aroused no interest and that no one turned to stare at me as a foreigner and stranger. I was utterly ignored, and my presence among them excited no special interest or attention.

'And then, quite suddenly, it dawned upon me with conviction that all the time this indifference and inattention were merely feigned. Everybody as a matter of fact was watching me closely. Every movement I made was known and observed. Ignoring me was all a pretence—an elaborate pretence.'

He paused a moment and looked at us to see if we were smiling, and then continued, reassured—

'It is useless to ask me how I noticed this, because I simply cannot explain it. But the discovery gave me something of a shock. Before I got back to the inn, however, another curious thing rose up strongly in my mind and forced my recognition of it as true. And this, too, I may as well say at once, was equally inexplicable to me. I mean I can only give you the fact, as fact it was to me.'

The little man left his chair and stood on the mat before the fire. His diffidence lessened from now onwards, as he lost himself again in the magic of the old adventure. His eyes shone a little already as he talked.

'Well,' he went on, his soft voice rising somewhat with his excitement, 'I was in a shop when it came to me first—though the idea must have been at work for a long time subconsciously to appear in so complete a form all at once. I was buying socks,

I think,' he laughed, 'and struggling with my dreadful French, when it struck me that the woman in the shop did not care two pins whether I bought anything or not. She was indifferent whether she made a sale or did not make a sale. She was only pretending to sell.

'This sounds a very small and fanciful incident to build upon what follows. But really it was not small. I mean it was the spark that lit the line of powder and ran along to the big blaze in my mind.

'For the whole town, I suddenly realised, was something other than I so far saw it. The real activities and interests of the people were elsewhere and otherwise than appeared. Their true lives lay somewhere out of sight behind the scenes. Their busyness was but the outward semblance that masked their actual purposes. They bought and sold, and ate and drank, and walked about the streets, yet all the while the main stream of their existence lay somewhere beyond my ken, underground, in secret places. In the shops and at the stalls they did not care whether I purchased their articles or not; at the inn, they were indifferent to my staying or going; their life lay remote from my own, springing from hidden, mysterious sources, coursing out of sight, unknown. It was all a great elaborate pretence, assumed possibly for my benefit, or possibly for purposes of their own. But the main current of their energies ran elsewhere. I almost felt as an unwelcome foreign substance might be expected to feel when it has found its way into the human system and the whole body organises itself to eject it or to absorb it. The town was doing this very thing to me.

'This bizarre notion presented itself forcibly to my mind as I walked home to the inn, and I began busily to wonder wherein the true life of this town could lie and what were the actual interests and activities of its hidden life.

'And, now that my eyes were partly opened, I noticed other things too that puzzled me, first of which, I think, was the extraordinary silence of the whole place. Positively, the town was muffled. Although the streets were paved with cobbles the people moved about silently, softly, with padded feet, like cats. Nothing made noise. All was hushed, subdued, muted. The very voices were quiet, low-pitched like purring. Nothing clamorous, vehement or emphatic seemed able to live in the drowsy atmosphere of soft dreaming that soothed this little hill-town into its sleep. It was like the woman at the inn—an outward repose screening intense inner activity and purpose.

'Yet there was no sign of lethargy or sluggishness anywhere about it. The people were active and alert. Only a magical and uncanny softness lay over them all like a spell.'

Vezin passed his hand across his eyes for a moment as though the memory had become very vivid. His voice had run off into a whisper so that we heard the last part with difficulty. He was telling a true thing obviously, yet something that he both liked and hated telling.

'I went back to the inn,' he continued presently in a louder voice, 'and dined. I felt a new strange world about me. My old world of reality receded. Here, whether I liked it or no, was something new and incomprehensible. I regretted having left the train so impulsively. An adventure was upon me, and I loathed adventures as foreign to my nature. Moreover, this was the beginning apparently of an adventure somewhere deep within me, in a region I could not check or measure, and a feeling of alarm mingled itself with my wonder—alarm for the stability of what I had for forty years recognised as my "personality".

'I went upstairs to bed, my mind teeming with thoughts that were unusual to me, and of rather a haunting description. By way of relief I kept thinking of that nice, prosaic noisy train and all those wholesome, blustering passengers. I almost wished I were with them again. But my dreams took me elsewhere. I dreamed of cats, and soft-moving creatures, and the silence of life in a dim muffled world beyond the senses.'

* * *

Vezin stayed on from day to day, indefinitely, much longer

than he had intended. He felt in a kind of dazed, somnolent condition. He did nothing in particular, but the place fascinated him and he could not decide to leave. Decisions were always very difficult for him and he sometimes wondered how he had ever brought himself to the point of leaving the train. It seemed as though someone else must have arranged it for him, and once or twice his thoughts ran to the swarthy Frenchman who had sat opposite. If only he could have understood that long sentence ending so strangely with '*à cause du sommeil et à cause des chats.*' He wondered what it all meant.

Meanwhile the hushed softness of the town held him prisoner and he sought in his muddling, gentle way to find out where the mystery lay, and what it was all about. But his limited French and his constitutional hatred of active investigation made it hard for him to buttonhole anybody and ask questions. He was content to observe, and watch, and remain negative.

The weather held on calm and hazy, and this just suited him. He wandered about the town till he knew every street and alley. The people suffered him to come and go without let or hindrance, though it became clearer to him every day that he was never free himself from observation. The town watched him as a cat watches a mouse. And he got no nearer to finding out what they were all so busy with or where the main stream of their activities lay. This remained hidden. The people were as soft and mysterious as cats.

But that he was continually under observation became more evident from day to day.

For instance, when he strolled to the end of the town and entered a little green public garden beneath the ramparts and seated himself upon one of the empty benches in the sun, he was quite alone—at first. Not another seat was occupied; the little park was empty, the paths deserted. Yet, within ten minutes of his coming, there must have been fully twenty persons scattered about him, some strolling aimlessly along the gravel walks, staring at the flowers, and others seated on the wooden benches enjoying the sun like himself. None of them appeared to take any notice of him; yet he understood quite well they had all come there to watch. They kept him under close observation. In the street they had seemed busy enough, hurrying upon various errands; yet these were suddenly all forgotten and they had nothing to do but loll and laze in the sun, their duties unremembered. Five minutes after he left, the garden was again deserted, the seats vacant. But in the crowded street it was the same thing again; he was never alone. He was ever in their thoughts.

By degrees, too, he began to see how it was he was so cleverly watched, yet without the appearance of it. The people did nothing *directly*. They behaved *obliquely*. He laughed in his mind as the thought thus clothed itself in words, but the phrase exactly described it. They looked at him from angles which naturally should have led their sight in another direction altogether. Their movements were oblique, too, so far as these concerned himself. The straight, direct thing was not their way evidently. They did nothing obviously. If he entered a shop to buy, the woman walked instantly away and busied herself with something at the farther end of the counter, though answering at once when he spoke, showing that she knew he was there and that this was only her way of attending to him. It was the fashion of the cat she followed. Even in the dining-room of the inn, the be-whiskered and courteous waiter, lithe and silent in all his movements, never seemed able to come straight to his table for an order or a dish. He came by zigzags, indirectly, vaguely, so that he appeared to be going to another table altogether, and only turned suddenly at the last moment, and was there beside him.

Vezin smiled curiously to himself as he described how he began to realise these things. Other tourists there were none in the hostel, but he recalled the figures of one or two old men, inhabitants, who took their *déjeuner* and dinner there, and remembered how fantastically they entered the room in similar fashion. First, they paused in the doorway, peering about the room, and then, after a temporary inspection, they came in, as it were, sideways, keeping close to the walls so that he wondered which table they were making for, and at the last minute making almost a little quick run to their particular seats. And again he thought of the ways and methods of cats.

Other small incidents, too, impressed him as all part of this queer, soft town with its muffled, indirect life, for the way some of the people appeared and disappeared with extraordinary swiftness puzzled him exceedingly. It may have been all perfectly natural, he knew, yet he could not make it out how the alleys swallowed them up and shot them forth in a second of time when there were no visible doorways or openings near enough to explain the phenomenon. Once he followed two elderly women who, he felt, had been particularly examining him from across the street—quite near the inn this was—and saw them turn the corner a few feet only in front of him. Yet when he sharply followed on their heels he saw nothing but an utterly deserted alley stretching in front of him with no sign of a living thing. And the only opening through which they could have escaped was a porch some fifty yards away, which not the swiftest human runner could have reached in time.

And in just such sudden fashion people appeared when he never expected them. Once when he heard a great noise of fighting going on behind a low wall, and hurried up to see what was going on, what should he see but a group of girls and women engaged in vociferous conversation which instantly hushed itself to the normal whispering note of the town when his head appeared over the wall. And even then none of them turned to look at him directly, but slunk off with the most unaccountable rapidity into doors and sheds across the yard. And their voices, he thought, had sounded so like, so strangely like, the angry snarling of fighting animals, almost of cats.

The whole spirit of the town, however, continued to evade him as something elusive, protean, screened from the outer world, and at the same time intensely, genuinely vital; and, since he now formed part of its life, this concealment puzzled and irritated him; more—it began rather to frighten him.

Out of the mists that slowly gathered about his ordinary surface thoughts, there rose again the idea that the inhabitants were waiting for him to declare himself, to take an attitude, to do this, or to do that; and that when he had done so they in their turn would at length make some direct response, accepting or rejecting him. Yet the vital matter concerning which his decision was awaited came no nearer to him.

Once or twice he purposely followed little processions or groups of the citizens in order to find out, if possible, on what purpose they were bent; but they always discovered him in time and dwindled away, each individual going his or her own way. It was always the same: he never could learn what their main interest was. The cathedral was ever empty, the old church of St. Martin, at the other end of the town, deserted. They shopped because they had to, and not because they wished to. The booths stood neglected, the stalls unvisited, the little cafés desolate. Yet the streets were always full, the townsfolk ever on the bustle.

'Can it be,' he thought to himself, yet with a deprecating laugh that he should have dared to think anything so odd, 'can it be that these people are people of the twilight, that they live only at night their real life, and come out honestly only with the dusk? That during the day they make a sham though brave pretence, and after the sun is down their true life begins? Have they the souls of night-things, and is the whole blessed town in the hands of the cats?'

The fancy somehow electrified him with little shocks of shrinking and dismay. Yet, though he affected to laugh, he knew that he was beginning to feel more than uneasy, and that strange forces were tugging with a thousand invisible cords at the very centre of his being. Something utterly remote from his ordinary life, something that had not waked for years, began faintly to stir in his soul, sending feelers abroad into his brain and heart, shaping queer thoughts and penetrating even into certain of his minor actions. Something exceedingly vital to himself, to his soul, hung in the balance.

And, always when he returned to the inn about the hour of sunset, he saw the figures of the townsfolk stealing through the dusk from their shop doors, moving sentry-wise to and fro at the corners of the streets, yet always vanishing silently like shadows at his near approach. And as the inn invariably closed its doors at ten o'clock he had never yet found the opportunity he rather half-heartedly sought to see for himself what account the town could give of itself at night.

'——*à cause du sommeil et à cause des chats*'—the words now rang in his ears more and more often, though still as yet without any definite meaning.

Moreover, something made him sleep like the dead.

* * *

It was, I think, on the fifth day—though in this detail his story sometimes varied—that he made a definite discovery which increased his alarm and brought him up to a rather sharp climax. Before that he had already noticed that a change was going forward and certain subtle transformations being brought about in his character which modified several of his minor habits. And he had affected to ignore them. Here, however, was something he could no longer ignore; and it startled him.

At the best of times he was never very positive, always negative rather, compliant and acquiescent; yet, when necessity arose he was capable of reasonably vigorous action and could take a strongish decision. The discovery he now made that brought him up with such a sharp turn was that this power had positively dwindled to nothing. He found it impossible to make up his mind. For, on this fifth day, he realised that he had stayed long enough in the town and that for reasons he could only vaguely define to himself it was wiser *and safer* that he should leave.

And he found that he could not leave!

This is difficult to describe in words, and it was more by

gesture and the expression of his face that he conveyed to Dr. Silence the state of impotence he had reached. All this spying and watching, he said, had as it were spun a net about his feet so that he was trapped and powerless to escape; he felt like a fly that had blundered into the intricacies of a great web; he was caught, imprisoned, and could not get away. It was a distressing sensation. A numbness had crept over his will till it had become almost incapable of decision. The mere thought of vigorous action—action towards escape—began to terrify him. All the currents of his life had turned inwards upon himself, striving to bring to the surface something that lay buried almost beyond reach, determined to force his recognition of something he had long forgotten—forgotten years upon years, centuries almost ago. It seemed as though a window deep within his being would presently open and reveal an entirely new world, yet somehow a world that was not unfamiliar. Beyond that, again, he fancied a great curtain hung; and when that too rolled up he would see still farther into this region and at last understand something of the secret life of these extraordinary people.

'Is this why they wait and watch?' he asked himself with rather a shaking heart, 'for the time when I shall join them—or refuse to join them? Does the decision rest with me after all, and not with them?'

And it was at this point that the sinister character of the adventure first really declared itself, and he became genuinely alarmed. The stability of his rather fluid little personality was at stake, he felt, and something in his heart turned coward.

Why otherwise should he have suddenly taken to walking stealthily, silently, making as little sound as possible, for ever looking behind him? Why else should he have moved almost on tiptoe about the passages of the practically deserted inn, and when he was abroad have found himself deliberately taking advantage of what cover presented itself? And why, if he was not afraid, should the wisdom of staying indoors after sundown have suddenly occurred to him as eminently desirable? Why, indeed?

And, when John Silence gently pressed him for an explanation of these things, he admitted apologetically that he had none to give.

'It was simply that I feared something might happen to me unless I kept a sharp look-out. I felt afraid. It was instinctive,' was all he could say. 'I got the impression that the whole town was after me—wanted me for something; and that if it got me I should lose myself, or at least the Self I knew, in some unfamiliar state of consciousness. But I am not a psychologist, you know,' he added meekly, 'and I cannot define it better than that.'

It was while lounging in the courtyard half an hour before the evening meal that Vezin made this discovery, and he at once went upstairs to his quiet room at the end of the winding passage to think it over alone. In the yard it was empty enough, true, but there was always the possibility that the big woman whom he dreaded would come out of some door, with her pretence of knitting, to sit and watch him. This had happened several times, and he could not endure the sight of her. He still remembered his original fancy, bizarre though it was, that she would spring upon him the moment his back was turned and land with one single crushing leap upon his neck. Of course it was nonsense, but then it haunted him, and once an idea begins to do that it ceases to be nonsense. It has clothed itself in reality.

He went upstairs accordingly. It was dusk, and the oil lamps had not yet been lit in the passages. He stumbled over the uneven surface of the ancient flooring, passing the dim outlines of doors along the corridor—doors that he had never once seen opened—rooms that seemed never occupied. He moved, as his habit now was, stealthily and on tiptoe.

Half-way down the last passage to his own chamber there was a sharp turn, and it was just here, while groping round the walls with outstretched hands, that his fingers touched something that was not wall—something that moved. It was soft and warm in texture, indescribably fragrant, and about the height of his shoulder; and he immediately thought of a furry, sweet-smelling kitten. The next minute he knew it was something quite different.

Instead of investigating, however—his nerves must have been too overwrought for that, he said—he shrank back as closely as possible against the wall on the other side. The thing, whatever it was, slipped past him with a sound of rustling, and retreating with light footsteps down the passage behind him, was gone. A breath of warm, scented air was wafted to his nostrils.

Vezin caught his breath for an instant and paused, stockstill, half leaning against the wall—and then almost ran down the remaining distance and entered his room with a rush, locking the door hurriedly behind him. Yet it was not fear that made him run: it was excitement, pleasurable excitement. His nerves were tingling, and a delicious glow made itself felt all over his body. In a flash it came to him that this was just what he had felt twenty-five years ago as a boy when he was in love for the first time. Warm currents of life ran all over him and mounted to his brain in a whirl of soft delight. His mood was suddenly become tender, melting, loving.

The room was quite dark, and he collapsed upon the sofa by the window, wondering what had happened to him and what it all meant. But the only thing he understood clearly in that instant was that something in him had swiftly, magically changed: he no longer wished to leave, or to argue with himself about leaving. The encounter in the passage-way had changed all that. The strange perfume of it still hung about him, bemusing his heart and mind. For he knew that it was a girl who had passed him, a girl's face that his fingers had brushed in the darkness, and he felt in some extraordinary way as though he had been actually kissed by her, kissed full upon the lips.

Trembling, he sat upon the sofa by the window and struggled to collect his thoughts. He was utterly unable to understand how the mere passing of a girl in the darkness of a narrow passage-way could communicate so electric a thrill to his whole being that he still shook with the sweetness of it. Yet, there it was! And he found it as useless to deny as to attempt analysis. Some ancient fire had entered his veins, and now ran coursing through his blood; and that he was forty-five instead of twenty did not matter one little jot. Out of all the inner turmoil and confusion emerged the one salient fact that the mere atmosphere, the merest casual touch, of this girl, unseen, unknown in the darkness, had been sufficient to stir dormant fires in the centre of his heart, and rouse his whole being from a state of feeble sluggishness to one of tearing and tumultuous excitement.

After a time, however, the number of Vezin's years began to assert their cumulative power; he grew calmer; and when a knock came at length upon his door and he heard the waiter's voice suggesting that dinner was nearly over, he pulled himself together and slowly made his way downstairs into the dining-room.

Everyone looked up as he entered, for he was very late, but he took his customary seat in the far corner and began to eat. The trepidation was still in his nerves, but the fact that he had passed through the courtyard and hall without catching sight of a petticoat served to calm him a little. He ate so fast that he had almost caught up with the current stage of the table d'hôte, when a slight commotion in the room drew his attention.

His chair was so placed that the door and the greater portion of the long *salle à manger* were behind him, yet it was not necessary to turn round to know that the same person he had passed in the dark passage had now come into the room. He felt the presence long before he heard or saw any one. Then he became aware that the old men, the only other guests, were rising one by one in their places, and exchanging greetings with someone who passed among them from table to table. And when at length he turned with his heart beating furiously to ascertain for himself, he saw the form of a young girl, lithe and slim, moving down the centre of the room and making straight for his own table in the corner. She moved wonderfully, with sinuous grace, like a young panther, and her approach filled him with such delicious bewilderment that he was utterly unable to tell at first what her face was like, or discover what it was about the whole presentment of the creature that filled him anew with trepidation and delight.

'Ah, Ma'mselle est de retour!" he heard the old waiter murmur at his side, and he was just able to take in that she was the daughter of the proprietress, when she was upon him, and he heard her voice. She was addressing him. Something of red lips he saw and laughing white teeth, and stray wisps of fine dark hair about the temples; but all the rest was a dream in which his own emotion rose like a thick cloud before his eyes and prevented his seeing accurately, or knowing exactly what he did. He was aware that she greeted him with a charming little bow; that her beautiful large eyes looked searchingly into his own; that the perfume he had noticed in the dark passage again assailed his nostrils, and that she was bending a little towards him and leaning with one hand on the table at his side. She was quite close to him—that was the chief thing he knew—explaining that she had been asking after the comfort of her mother's guests, and was now introducing herself to the latest arrival—himself.

'M'sieur has already been here a few days,' he heard the waiter say; and then her own voice, sweet as singing, replied—

'Ah, but M'sieur is not going to leave us just yet, I hope. My mother is too old to look after the comfort of our guests properly, but now I am here I will remedy all that.' She laughed deliciously. 'M'sieur shall be well looked after.'

Vezin, struggling with his emotion and desire to be polite, half rose to acknowledge the pretty speech, and to stammer some sort of reply, but as he did so his hand by chance touched her own that was resting upon the table, and a shock that was for all the world like a shock of electricity, passed from her skin into his body. His soul wavered and shook deep within him. He caught her eyes fixed upon his own with a look of most curious intentness, and the next moment he knew that he had sat down wordless again on his chair, that the girl was already half-way across the room, and that he was trying to eat his salad with a dessert-spoon and a knife.

Longing for her return, and yet dreading it, he gulped down the remainder of his dinner, and then went at once to his bedroom to be alone with his thoughts. This time the passages were lighted, and he suffered no exciting contretemps; yet the winding corridor was dim with shadows, and the last portion, from the bend of the walls onwards, seemed longer than he had ever known it. It ran downhill like the pathway on a mountain side, and as he tiptoed softly down it he felt that by rights it ought to have led him clean out of the house into the heart of a great forest. The world was singing with him. Strange fancies filled his brain, and once in the room, with the door securely locked, he did not light the candles, but sat by the open window thinking long, long thoughts that came unbidden in troops to his mind.

*　　*　　*

This part of the story he told to Dr. Silence, without special coaxing, it is true, yet with much stammering embarrassment. He could not in the least understand, he said, how the girl had managed to affect him so profoundly, and even before he had set eyes upon her. For her mere proximity in the darkness had been sufficient to set him on fire. He knew nothing of enchantments, and for years had been a stranger to anything approaching tender relations with any member of the opposite sex, for he was encased in shyness, and realised his overwhelming defects only too well. Yet this bewitching young creature came to him deliberately. Her manner was unmistakable, and she sought him out on every possible occasion. Chaste and sweet she was undoubtedly, yet frankly inviting; and she won him utterly with the first glance of her shining eyes, even if she had not already done so in the dark merely by the magic of her invisible presence.

'You felt she was altogether wholesome and good?' queried the doctor. 'You had no reaction of any sort—for instance, of alarm?'

Vezin looked up sharply with one of his inimitable little apologetic smiles. It was some time before he replied. The mere memory of the adventure had suffused his shy face with blushes, and his brown eyes sought the floor again before he answered.

'I don't think I can quite say that,' he explained presently. 'I acknowledged certain qualms, sitting up in my room afterwards. A conviction grew upon me that there was something about her—how shall I express it?—well, something unholy. It is not impurity in any sense, physical or mental, that I mean, but something quite indefinable that gave me a vague sensation of the creeps. She drew me, and at the same time repelled me, more than—than——'

He hesitated, blushing furiously, and unable to finish the sentence.

'Nothing like it has ever come to me before or since,' he concluded, with lame confusion. 'I suppose it was, as you suggested just now, something of an enchantment. At any rate, it was strong enough to make me feel that I would stay in that awful little haunted town for years if only I could see her every day, hear her voice, watch her wonderful movements, and sometimes, perhaps, touch her hand.'

'Can you explain to me what you felt was the source of her power?' John Silence asked, looking purposely anywhere but at the narrator.

'I am surprised that *you* should ask me such a question,' answered Vezin, with the nearest approach to dignity he could manage. 'I think no man can describe to another convincingly wherein lies the magic of the woman who ensnares him. I certainly cannot. I can only say this slip of a girl bewitched me, and the mere knowledge that she was living and sleeping in the same house filled me with an extraordinary sense of delight.

'But there's one thing I can tell you,' he went on earnestly, his eyes aglow, 'namely, that she seemed to sum up and synthesise in herself all the strange hidden forces that operated so mysteriously in the town and its inhabitants. She had the silken movements of the panther, going smoothly, silently to and fro, and the same indirect, oblique methods as the townsfolk, screening, like them, secret purposes of her own—purposes that I was sure had *me* for their objective. She kept me, to my terror and delight, ceaselessly under observation, yet so carelessly, so consummately, that another man less sensitive, if I may say so'—he made a deprecating gesture—'or less prepared by what had gone before, would never have noticed it at all. She was always still, always reposeful, yet she seemed to be everywhere at once, so that I never could escape from her. I was continually meeting the stare and laughter of her great eyes, in the corners of the rooms, in the passages, calmly looking at me through the windows, or in the busiest parts of the public streets.'

Their intimacy, it seems, grew very rapidly after this first encounter which had so violently disturbed the little man's equilibrium. He was naturally very prim, and prim folk live mostly in so small a world that anything violently unusual may shake them clean out of it, and they therefore instinctively distrust originality. But Vezin began to forget his primness after awhile. The girl was always modestly behaved, and as her mother's representative she naturally had to do with the guests in the hotel. It was not out of the way that a spirit of camaraderie should spring up. Besides, she was young, she was charmingly pretty, she was French, and—she obviously liked him.

At the same time, there was something indescribable—a certain indefinable atmosphere of other places, other times—that made him try hard to remain on his guard, and sometimes made him catch his breath with a sudden start. It was all rather like a delirious dream, half delight, half dread, he confided in a whisper to Dr. Silence; and more than once he hardly knew quite what he was doing or saying, as though he were driven forward by impulses he scarcely recognised as his own.

And though the thought of leaving presented itself again and again to his mind, it was each time with less insistence, so that he stayed on from day to day, becoming more and more a part of the sleepy life of this dreamy mediæval town, losing more and more of his recognisable personality. Soon, he felt, the Curtain within would roll up with an awful rush, and he would find himself suddenly admitted into the secret purposes of the hidden life that lay behind it all. Only, by that time, he would have become transformed into an entirely different being.

And, meanwhile, he noticed various little signs of the intention to make his stay attractive to him: flowers in his bedroom, a more comfortable arm-chair in the corner, and even special little extra dishes on his private table in the dining-room. Conversations, too, with 'Mademoiselle Ilsé' became more and more frequent and pleasant, and although they seldom travelled beyond the weather, or the details of the town, the girl, he noticed, was never in a hurry to bring them to an end, and often contrived to interject little odd sentences that he never properly understood, yet felt to be significant.

And it was these stray remarks, full of a meaning that evaded him, that pointed to some hidden purpose of her own and made him feel uneasy. They all had to do, he felt sure, with reasons for his staying on in the town indefinitely.

'And has M'sieur not even yet come to a decision?' she said softly in his ear, sitting beside him in the sunny yard before *déjeuner*, the acquaintance having progressed with significant rapidity. 'Because, if it's so difficult, we must all try together to help him!'

The question startled him, following upon his own thoughts. It was spoken with a pretty laugh, and a stray bit of hair across one eye, as she turned and peered at him half roguishly.

Possibly he did not quite understand the French of it, for her near presence always confused his small knowledge of the language distressingly. Yet the words, and her manner, and something else that lay behind it all in her mind, frightened him. It gave such point to his feeling that the town was waiting for him to make his mind up on some important matter.

At the same time, her voice, and the fact that she was there so close beside him in her soft dark dress, thrilled him inexpressibly.

'It is true I find it difficult to leave,' he stammered, losing his way deliciously in the depths of her eyes, 'and especially now that Mademoiselle Ilsé has come.'

He was surprised at the success of his sentence, and quite delighted with the little gallantry of it. But at the same time he could have bitten his tongue off for having said it.

'Then after all you like our little town, or you would not be pleased to stay on,' she said, ignoring the compliment .

'I am enchanted with it, and enchanted with you,' he cried, feeling that his tongue was somehow slipping beyond the control of his brain. And he was on the verge of saying all manner of other things of the wildest description, when the girl sprang lightly up from her chair beside him, and made to go.

'It is *soupe à l'onion* today!' she cried, laughing back at him through the sunlight, 'and I must go and see about it. Otherwise, you know, M'sieur will not enjoy his dinner, and then, perhaps, he will leave us!'

He watched her cross the courtyard, moving with all the grace and lightness of the feline race, and her simple black dress clothed her, he thought, exactly like the fur of the same supple species. She turned once to laugh at him from the porch with the glass door, and then stopped a moment to speak to her mother, who sat knitting as usual in her corner seat just inside the hall-way.

But how was it, then, that the moment his eye fell upon this ungainly woman, the pair of them appeared suddenly as other than they were? Whence came that transforming dignity and sense of power that enveloped them both as by magic? What was it about that massive woman that made her appear instantly regal, and set her on a throne in some dark and dreadful scenery, wielding a sceptre over the red glare of some tempestuous orgy? And why did this slender stripling of a girl, graceful as a willow, lithe as a young leopard, assume suddenly an air of sinister majesty, and move with flame and smoke about her head, and the darkness of night beneath her feet?

Vezin caught his breath and sat there transfixed. Then, almost simultaneously with its appearance, the queer notion vanished again, and the sunlight of day caught them both, and he heard her laughing to her mother about the *soupe à l'onion*, and saw her glancing back at him over her dear little shoulder with a smile that made him think of a dew-kissed rose bending lightly before summer airs.

And, indeed, the onion soup was particularly excellent that day, because he saw another cover laid at his small table and, with fluttering heart, heard the waiter murmur by way of explanation that 'Ma'mselle Ilsé would honour M'sieur today at *déjeuner*, as her custom sometimes is with her mother's guests.'

So actually she sat by him all through that delirious meal, talking quietly to him in easy French, seeing that he was well looked after, mixing the salad-dressing, and even helping him with her own hand. And, later in the afternoon, while he was smoking in the courtyard, longing for a sight of her as soon as her duties were done, she came again to his side, and when he rose to meet her, she stood facing him a moment, full of a perplexing sweet shyness before she spoke—

'My mother thinks you ought to know more of the beauties of our little town, and *I* think so too! Would M'sieur like me to be his guide, perhaps? I can show him everything, for our family has lived here for many generations.'

She had him by the hand, indeed, before he could find a single word to express his pleasure, and led him, all unresisting, out into the street, yet in such a way that it seemed perfectly natural she should do so, and without the faintest suggestion of boldness or immodesty. Her face glowed with the pleasure and interest of it, and with her short dress and tumbled hair she looked every bit the charming child of seventeen that she was, innocent and playful, proud of her native town, and alive beyond her years to the sense of its ancient beauty.

So they went over the town together, and she showed him what she considered its chief interest: the tumble-down old house where her forebears had lived; the sombre, aristocratic-looking mansion where her mother's family dwelt for centuries, and the ancient market-place where several hundred years before the witches had been burnt by the score. She kept up a lively running stream of talk about it all, of which he understood not a fiftieth part as he trudged along by her side, cursing his forty-five years and feeling all the yearnings of his early manhood revive and jeer at him. And, as she talked, England and Surbiton seemed very far away indeed, almost in another age of the world's history. Her voice touched something immeasurably old in him, something that slept deep. It lulled the surface parts of his consciousness to sleep, allowing what was far more ancient to awaken. Like the town, with its elaborate pretence of modern active life, the upper layers of his being became dulled, soothed, muffled, and what lay underneath began to stir in its sleep. That big Curtain swayed a little to and fro. Presently it might lift altogether. . . .

He began to understand a little better at last. The mood of the town was reproducing itself in him. In proportion as his ordinary external self became muffled, that inner secret life, that was far more real and vital, asserted itself. And this girl was surely the high-priestess of it all, the chief instrument of its accomplishment. New thoughts, with new interpretations, flooded his mind as she walked beside him through the winding streets, while the picturesque old gabled town, softly coloured in the sunset, had never appeared to him so wholly wonderful and seductive.

And only one curious incident came to disturb and puzzle

him, slight in itself, but utterly inexplicable, bringing white terror into the child's face and a scream to her laughing lips. He had merely pointed to a column of blue smoke that rose from the burning autumn leaves and made a picture against the red roofs, and had then run to the wall and called her to his side to watch the flames shooting here and there through the heap of rubbish. Yet, at the sight of it, as though taken by surprise, her face had altered dreadfully, and she had turned and run like the wind, calling out wild sentences to him as she ran, of which he had not understood a single word, except that the fire apparently frightened her, and she wanted to get quickly away from it, and to get him away too.

Yet five minutes later she was as calm and happy again as though nothing had happened to alarm or waken troubled thoughts in her, and they had both forgotten the incident.

They were leaning over the ruined ramparts together listening to the weird music of the band as he had heard it the first day of his arrival. It moved him again profoundly as it had done before, and somehow he managed to find his tongue and his best French. The girl leaned across the stones close beside him. No one was about. Driven by some remorseless engine within he began to stammer something—he hardly knew what—of his strange admiration for her. Almost at the first word she sprang lightly off the wall and came up smiling in front of him, just touching his knees as he sat there. She was hatless as usual, and the sun caught her hair and one side of her cheek and throat.

'Oh, I'm *so* glad!' she cried, clapping her little hands softly in his face, 'so very glad, because that means that if you like me you must also like what I do, and what I belong to.'

Already he regretted bitterly having lost control of himself. Something in the phrasing of her sentence chilled him. He knew the fear of embarking upon an unknown and dangerous sea.

'You will take part in our real life, I mean,' she added softly, with an indescribable coaxing of manner, as though she noticed his shrinking. 'You will come back to us.'

Already this slip of a child seemed to dominate him; he felt her power coming over him more and more; something emanated from her that stole over his senses and made him aware that her personality, for all its simple grace, held forces that were stately, imposing, august. He saw her again moving through smoke and flame amid broken and tempestuous scenery, alarmingly strong, her terrible mother by her side. Dimly this shone through her smile and appearance of charming innocence.

'You will, I know," she repeated, holding him with her eyes.

They were quite alone up there on the ramparts, and the sensation that she was overmastering him stirred a wild sensuousness in his blood. The mingled abandon and reserve in her attracted him furiously, and all of him that was man rose up and resisted the creeping influence, at the same time acclaiming it with the full delight of his forgotten youth. An irresistible desire came to him to question her, to summon what still remained to him of his own little personality in an effort to retain the right to his normal self.

The girl had grown quiet again, and was now leaning on the broad wall close beside him, gazing out across the darkening plain, her elbows on the coping, motionless as a figure carved in stone. He took his courage in both hands.

'Tell me, Ilsé,' he said, unconsciously imitating her own purring softness of voice, yet aware that he was utterly in earnest, 'what is the meaning of this town, and what is this real life you speak of? And why is it that the people watch me from morning to night? Tell me what it all means? And, tell me,' he added more quickly with passion in his voice, 'what you really are—yourself?'

She turned her head and looked at him through half-closed eyelids, her growing inner excitement betraying itself by the faint colour that ran like a shadow across her face.

'It seems to me,'—he faltered oddly under her gaze—'that I have some right to know——'

Suddenly she opened her eyes to the full. 'You love me, then?' she asked softly.

'I swear,' he cried impetuously, moved as by the force of a rising tide, 'I never felt before—I have never known any other girl who——'

'Then you *have* the right to know,' she calmly interrupted his confused confession; 'for love shares all secrets.'

She paused, and a thrill like fire ran swiftly through him. Her words lifted him off the earth, and he felt a radiant happiness, followed almost the same instant in horrible contrast by the thought of death. He became aware that she had turned her eyes upon his own and was speaking again.

'The real life I speak of,' she whispered, 'is the old, old life within, the life of long ago, the life to which you, too, once belonged, and to which you still belong.'

A faint wave of memory troubled the deeps of his soul as her low voice sank into him. What she was saying he knew instinctively to be true, even though he could not as yet understand its full purport. His present life seemed slipping from him as he listened, merging his personality in one that was far older and greater. It was this loss of his present self that brought to him the thought of death.

'You came here,' she went on, 'with the purpose of seeking it, and the people felt your presence and are waiting to know what you decide, whether you will leave them without having found it, or whether——'

Her eyes remained fixed upon his own, but her face began to change, growing larger and darker with an expression of age.

'It is their thoughts constantly playing about your soul that makes you feel they watch you. They do not watch you with their eyes. The purposes of their inner life are calling to you, seeking to claim you. You were all part of the same life long, long ago, and now they want you back again among them.'

Vezin's timid heart sank with dread as he listened; but the girl's eyes held him with a net of joy so that he had no wish to escape. She fascinated him, as it were, clean out of his normal self.

'Alone, however, the people could never have caught and held you,' she resumed. 'The motive force was not strong enough; it has faded through all these years. But I'—she paused a moment and looked at him with complete confidence in her splendid eyes—'I possess the spell to conquer you and hold you: the spell of old love. I can win you back again and make you live the old life with me, for the force of the ancient tie between us, if I choose to use it, is irresistible. And I do choose to use it. I still want you. And you, dear soul of my dim past'—she pressed closer to him so that her breath passed across his eyes, and her voice positively sang—'I mean to have you, for you love me and are utterly at my mercy.'

Vezin heard, and yet did not hear; understood, yet did not understand. He had passed into a condition of exaltation. The world was beneath his feet, made of music and flowers, and he was flying somewhere far above it through the sunshine of pure delight. He was breathless and giddy with the wonder of her words. They intoxicated him. And, still, the terror of it all, the dreadful thought of death, pressed ever behind her sentences. For flames shot through her voice out of black smoke and licked at his soul.

And they communicated with one another, it seemed to him, by a process of swift telepathy, for his French could never have compassed all he said to her. Yet she understood perfectly, and what she said to him was like the recital of verses long since known. And the mingled pain and sweetness of it as he listened were almost more than his little soul could hold.

'Yet I came here wholly by chance——' he heard himself saying.

'No,' she cried with passion, 'you came here because I called to you. I have called to you for years, and you came with the whole force of the past behind you. You had to come, for I own you, and I claim you.'

She rose again and moved closer, looking at him with a

certain insolence in the face—the insolence of power.

The sun had set behind the towers of the old cathedral and the darkness rose up from the plain and enveloped them. The music of the band had ceased. The leaves of the plane trees hung motionless, but the chill of the autumn evening rose about them and made Vezin shiver. There was no sound but the sound of their voices and the occasional soft rustle of the girl's dress. He could hear the blood rushing in his ears. He scarcely realised where he was or what he was doing. Some terrible magic of the imagination drew him deeply down into the tombs of his own being, telling him in no unfaltering voice that her words shadowed forth the truth. And this simple little French maid, speaking beside him with so strange authority, he saw curiously alter into quite another being. As he stared into her eyes, the picture in his mind grew and lived, dressing itself vividly to his inner vision with a degree of reality he was compelled to acknowledge. As once before, he saw her tall and stately, moving through wild and broken scenery of forests and mountain caverns, the glare of flames behind her head and clouds of shifting smoke about her feet. Dark leaves encircled her hair, flying loosely in the wind, and her limbs shone through the merest rags of clothing. Others were about her too, and ardent eyes on all sides cast delirious glances upon her, but her own eyes were always for One only, one whom she held by the hand. For she was leading the dance in some tempestuous orgy to the music of chanting voices, and the dance she led circled about a great and awful Figure on a throne, brooding over the scene through lurid vapours, while innumerable other wild faces and forms crowded furiously about her in the dance. But the one she held by the hand he knew to be himself, and the monstrous shape upon the throne he knew to be her mother.

The vision rose within him, rushing to him down the long years of buried time, crying aloud to him with the voice of memory reawakened. . . . And then the scene faded away and he saw the clear circle of the girl's eyes gazing steadfastly into his own, and she became once more the pretty little daughter of the innkeeper, and he found his voice again.

'And you,' he whispered tremblingly—'you child of visions and enchantment, how is it that you so bewitch me that I loved you even before I saw?'

She drew herself up beside him with an air of rare dignity.

'The call of the Past,' she said; 'and besides,' she added proudly, 'in the real life I am a princess——'

'A princess!' he cried.

'——and my mother is a queen!'

At this, little Vezin utterly lost his head. Delight tore at his heart and swept him into sheer ecstasy. To hear that sweet singing voice, and to see those adorable little lips utter such things, upset his balance beyond all hope of control. He took her in his arms and covered her unresisting face with kisses.

But even while he did so, and while the hot passion swept him, he felt that she was soft and loathsome, and that her answering kisses stained his very soul. . . . And when, presently, she had freed herself and vanished into the darkness, he stood there, leaning against the wall in a state of collapse, creeping with horror from the touch of her yielding body, and inwardly raging at the weakness that he already dimly realised must prove his undoing.

And from the shadows of the old buildings into which she disappeared there rose in the stillness of the night a singular, long-drawn cry, which at first he took for laughter, but which later he was sure he recognised as the almost human wailing of a cat.

* * *

For a long time Vezin leant there against the wall, alone with his surging thoughts and emotions. He understood at length that he had done the one thing necessary to call down upon him the whole force of this ancient Past. For in those passionate kisses he had acknowledged the tie of olden days, and had revived it. And the memory of that soft impalpable caress in the darkness of the inn corridor came back to him with a shudder. The girl had first mastered him, and then led him to the one act that was necessary for her purpose. He had been waylaid, after the lapse of centuries—caught, and conquered.

Dimly he realised this, and sought to make plans for his escape. But, for the moment at any rate, he was powerless to manage his thoughts or will, for the sweet, fantastic madness of the whole adventure mounted to his brain like a spell, and he gloried in the feeling that he was utterly enchanted and moving in a world so much larger and wilder than the one he had ever been accustomed to.

The moon, pale and enormous, was just rising over the sea-like plain, when at last he rose to go. Her slanting rays drew all the houses into new perspective, so that their roofs, already glistening with dew, seemed to stretch much higher into the sky than usual, and their gables and quaint old towers lay far away in its purple reaches.

The cathedral appeared unreal in a silver mist. He moved softly, keeping to the shadows; but the streets were all deserted and very silent; the doors were closed, the shutters fastened. Not a soul was astir. The hush of night lay over everything; it was like a town of the dead, a churchyard with gigantic and grotesque tombstones.

Wondering where all the busy life of the day had so utterly disappeared to, he made his way to a back door that entered the inn by means of the stables, thinking thus to reach his room unobserved. He reached the courtyard safely and crossed it by keeping close to the shadow of the wall. He sidled down it, mincing along on tiptoe, just as the old men did when they entered the *salle à manger*. He was horrified to find himself doing this instinctively. A strange impulse came to him, catching him somehow in the centre of his body—an impulse to drop upon all fours and run swiftly and silently. He glanced upwards and the idea came to him to leap up upon his window-sill overhead instead of going round by the stairs. This occurred to him as the easiest, and most natural way. It was like the beginning of some horrible transformation of himself into something else. He was fearfully strung up.

The moon was higher now, and the shadows very dark along the side of the street where he moved. He kept among the deepest of them, and reached the porch with the glass doors.

But here there was light; the inmates, unfortunately, were still about. Hoping to slip across the hall unobserved and reach the stairs, he opened the door carefully and stole in. Then he saw that the hall was not empty. A large dark thing lay against the wall on his left. At first he thought it must be household articles. Then it moved, and he thought it was an immense cat, distorted in some way by the play of light and shadow. Then it rose straight up before him and he saw that it was the proprietress.

What she had been doing in this position he could only venture a dreadful guess, but the moment she stood up and faced him he was aware of some terrible dignity clothing her about that instantly recalled the girl's strange saying that she was a queen. Huge and sinister she stood there under the little oil lamp; alone with him in the empty hall. Awe stirred in his heart, and the roots of some ancient fear. He felt that he must bow to her and make some kind of obeisance. The impulse was fierce and irresistible, as of long habit. He glanced quickly about him. There was no one there. Then he deliberately inclined his head towards her. He bowed.

'Enfin! M'sieur s'est donc décidé. C'est bien alors. J'en suis contente.'

Her words came to him sonorously as through a great open space.

Then the great figure came suddenly across the flagged hall at him and seized his trembling hands. Some overpowering force moved with her and caught him.

'On pourrait faire un p'tit ensemble, n'est-ce pas? Nous y allons cette nuit et il faut s'exercer un peu d'avance pour cela.

Ilsé, Ilsé, viens donc ici. Viens vite!'

And she whirled him round in the opening steps of some dance that seemed oddly and horribly familiar. They made no sound on the stones, this strangely assorted couple. It was all soft and stealthy. And, presently, when the air seemed to thicken like smoke, and a red glare as of flame shot through it, he was aware that someone else had joined them and that his hand the mother had released was now tightly held by the daughter. Ilsé had come in answer to the call, and he saw her with leaves of vervain twined in her dark hair, clothed in tattered vestiges of some curious garment, beautiful as the night, and horribly, odiously, loathsomely seductive.

'To the Sabbath! to the Sabbath!' they cried. 'On to the Witches' Sabbath!'

Up and down that narrow hall they danced, the women on each side of him, to the wildest measure he had ever imagined, yet which he dimly, dreadfully remembered, till the lamp on the wall flickered and went out, and they were left in total darkness. And the devil woke in his heart with a thousand vile suggestions and made him afraid.

Suddenly they released his hands and he heard the voice of the mother cry that it was time, and they must go. Which way they went he did not pause to see. He only realised that he was free, and he blundered through the darkness till he found the stairs and then tore up them to his room as though all hell was at his heels.

He flung himself on the sofa, with his face in his hands, and groaned. Swiftly reviewing a dozen ways of immediate escape, all equally impossible, he finally decided that the only thing to do for the moment was to sit quiet and wait. He must see what was going to happen. At least in the privacy of his own bedroom he would be fairly safe. The door was locked. He crossed over and softly opened the window which gave upon the courtyard and also permitted a partial view of the hall through the glass doors.

As he did so the hum and murmur of a great activity

reached his ears from the streets beyond—the sound of footsteps and voices muffled by distance. He leaned out cautiously and listened. The moonlight was clear and strong now, but his own window was in shadow, the silver disc being still behind the house. It came to him irresistibly that the inhabitants of the town, who a little while before had all been invisible behind closed doors, were now issuing forth, busy upon some secret and unholy errand. He listened intently.

At first everything about him was silent, but soon he became aware of movements going on in the house itself. Rustlings and cheepings came to him across that still, moonlit yard. A concourse of living beings sent the hum of their activity into the night. Things were on the move everywhere. A biting, pungent odour rose through the air, coming he knew not whence. Presently his eyes became glued to the windows of the opposite wall where the moonshine fell in a soft blaze. The roof overhead, and behind him, was reflected clearly in the panes of glass, and he saw the outlines of dark bodies moving with long footsteps over the tiles and along the coping. They passed swiftly and silently, shaped like immense cats, in an endless procession across the pictured glass, and then appeared to leap down to a lower level where he lost sight of them. He just caught the soft thudding of their leaps. Sometimes their shadows fell upon the white wall opposite, and then he could not make out whether they were the shadows of human beings or of cats. They seemed to change swiftly from one to the other. The transformation looked horribly real, for they leaped like human beings, yet changed swiftly in the air immediately afterwards, and dropped like animals.

The yard, too, beneath him, was now alive with the creeping movements of dark forms all stealthily drawing towards the porch with the glass doors. They kept so closely to the wall that he could not determine their actual shape, but when he saw that they passed on to the great congregation that was gathering in the hall, he understood that these were the creatures whose leaping shadows he had first seen reflected in the window-panes opposite. They were coming from all parts of the town, reaching the appointed meeting-place across the roofs and tiles, and springing from level to level till they came to the yard.

Then a new sound caught his ear, and he saw that the windows all about him were being softly opened, and that to each window came a face. A moment later figures began dropping hurriedly down into the yard. And these figures, as they lowered themselves down from the windows, were human, he saw; but once safely in the yard they fell upon all fours and changed in the swiftest possible second into—cats—huge, silent cats. They ran in streams to join the main body in the hall beyond.

So, after all, the rooms in the house had not been empty and unoccupied.

Moreover, what he saw no longer filled him with amazement. For he remembered it all. It was familiar. It had all happened before just so, hundreds of times, and he himself had taken part in it and known the wild madness of it all. The outline of the old building changed, the yard grew larger, and he seemed to be staring down upon it from a much greater height through smoky vapours. And, as he looked, half remembering, the old pains of long ago, fierce and sweet, furiously assailed him, and the blood stirred horribly as he heard the Call of the Dance again in his heart and tasted the ancient magic of Ilsé whirling by his side.

Suddenly he started back. A great lithe cat had leaped softly up from the shadows below on to the sill close to his face, and was staring fixedly at him with the eyes of a human. 'Come,' it seemed to say, 'come with us to the Dance! Change as of old! Transform yourself swiftly and come!' Only too well he understood the creature's soundless call.

It was gone again in a flash with scarcely a sound of its padded feet on the stones, and then others dropped by the score down the side of the house, past his very eyes, all changing as they fell and darting away rapidly, softly, towards the gathering point. And again he felt the dreadful desire to do likewise; to murmur the old incantation, and then drop upon hands and knees and run swiftly for the great flying leap into the air. Oh, how the passion of it rose within him like a flood, twisting his very entrails, sending his heart's desire flaming forth into the night for the old, old Dance of the Sorcerers at the Witches' Sabbath! The whirl of the stars was about him; once more he met the magic of the moon. The power of the wind, rushing from precipice and forest, leaping from cliff to cliff across the valleys, tore him away.... He heard the cries of the dancers and their wild laughter, and with this savage girl in his embrace he danced furiously about the dim Throne where sat the Figure with the sceptre of majesty....

Then, suddenly, all became hushed and still, and the fever died down a little in his heart. The calm moonlight flooded a courtyard empty and deserted. They had started. The procession was off into the sky. And he was left behind—alone.

Vezin tiptoed softly across the room and unlocked the door. The murmur from the streets, growing momentarily as he advanced, met his ears. He made his way with the utmost caution down the corridor. At the head of the stairs he paused and listened. Below him, the hall where they had gathered was dark and still, but through opened doors and windows on the far side of the building came the sound of a great throng moving farther and farther into the distance.

He made his way down the creaking wooden stairs, dreading yet longing to meet some straggler who should point the way, but finding no one; across the dark hall, so lately thronged with living, moving things, and out through the opened front doors into the street. He could not believe that he was really left behind, really forgotten, that he had been purposely permitted to escape. It perplexed him.

Nervously he peered about him, and up and down the street; then, seeing nothing, advanced slowly down the pavement.

The whole town, as he went, showed itself empty and

deserted, as though a great wind had blown everything alive out of it. The doors and windows of the houses stood open to the night; nothing stirred; moonlight and silence lay over all. The night lay about him like a cloak. The air, soft and cool, caressed his cheek like the touch of a great furry paw. He gained confidence and began to walk quickly, though still keeping to the shadowed side. Nowhere could he discover the faintest sign of the great unholy exodus he knew had just taken place. The moon sailed high over all in a sky, cloudless and serene.

Hardly realising where he was going, he crossed the open market-place and so came to the ramparts, whence he knew a pathway descended to the high road and along which he could make good his escape to one of the other little towns that lay to the northward, and so to the railway.

But first he paused and gazed out over the scene at his feet where the great plain lay like a silver map of some dream country. The still beauty of it entered his heart, increasing his sense of bewilderment and unreality. No air stirred, the leaves of the plane trees stood motionless, the near details were defined with the sharpness of day against dark shadows, and in the distance the fields and woods melted away into haze and shimmering mistiness.

But the breath caught in his throat and he stood stockstill as though transfixed when his gaze passed from the horizon and fell upon the near prospect in the depth of the valley at his feet. The whole lower slopes of the hill, that lay hid from the brightness of the moon, were aglow, and through the glare he saw countless moving forms, shifting thick and fast between the openings of the trees; while overhead, like leaves driven by the wind, he discerned flying shapes that hovered darkly one moment against the sky and then settled down with cries and weird singing through the branches into the region that was aflame.

Spellbound, he stood and stared for a time that he could not measure. And then, moved by one of the terrible impulses that seemed to control the whole adventure, he climbed swiftly upon the top of the broad coping, and balanced a moment where the valley gaped at his feet. But in that very instant, as he stood hovering, a sudden movement among the shadows of the houses caught his eye, and he turned to see the outline of a large animal dart swiftly across the open space behind him, and land with a flying leap upon the top of the wall a little lower down. It ran like the wind to his feet and then rose up beside him upon the ramparts. A shiver seemed to run through the moonlight, and his sight trembled for a second. His heart pulsed fearfully. Ilsé stood beside him, peering into his face.

Some dark substance, he saw, stained the girl's face and skin, shining in the moonlight as she stretched her hands towards him; she was dressed in wretched tattered garments that yet became her mightily; rue and vervain twined about her temples; her eyes glittered with unholy light. He only just controlled the wild impulse to take her in his arms and leap with her from their giddy perch into the valley below.

'See!' she cried, pointing with an arm on which the rags fluttered in the rising wind towards the forest aglow in the distance. 'See where they await us! The woods are alive! Already the Great Ones are there, and the dance will soon begin! The salve is here! Anoint yourself and come!'

Though a moment before the sky was clear and cloudless, yet even while she spoke the face of the moon grew dark and the wind began to toss in the crests of the plane trees at his feet. Stray gusts brought the sounds of hoarse singing and crying from the lower slopes of the hill, and the pungent odour he had already noticed about the courtyard of the inn rose about him in the air.

'Transform, transform!' she cried again, her voice rising like a song. 'Rub well your skin before you fly. Come! Come with me to the Sabbath, to the madness of its furious delight, to the sweet abandonment of its evil worship! See! the Great Ones are there, and the terrible Sacraments prepared. The

Throne is occupied. Anoint and come! Anoint and come!'

She grew to the height of a tree beside him, leaping upon the wall with flaming eyes and hair strewn upon the night. He too began to change swiftly. Her hands touched the skin of his face and neck, streaking him with the burning salve that sent the old magic into his blood with the power before which fades all that is good.

A wild roar came up to his ears from the heart of the wood, and the girl, when she heard it, leaped upon the wall in the frenzy of her wicked joy.

'Satan is there!' she screamed, rushing upon him and striving to draw him with her to the edge of the wall. 'Satan has come! The Sacraments call us! Come, with your dear apostate soul, and we will worship and dance till the moon dies and the world is forgotten!'

Just saving himself from the dreadful plunge, Vezin struggled to release himself from her grasp, while the passion tore at his reins and all but mastered him. He shrieked aloud, not knowing what he said, and then he shrieked again. It was the old impulses, the old awful habits instinctively finding voice; for though it seemed to him that he merely shrieked nonsense, the words he uttered really had meaning in them, and were intelligible. It was the ancient call. And it was heard below. It was answered.

The wind whistled at the skirts of his coat as the air round him darkened with many flying forms crowding upwards out of the valley. The crying of hoarse voices smote upon his ears, coming closer. Strokes of wind buffeted him, tearing him this way and that along the crumbling top of the stone wall; and Ilsé clung to him with her long shining arms, smooth and bare, holding him fast about the neck. But not Ilsé alone, for a dozen of them surrounded him, dropping out of the air. The pungent odour of the anointed bodies stifled him, exciting him to the old madness of the Sabbath, the dance of the witches and sorcerers doing honour to the personified Evil of the world.

'Anoint and away! Anoint and away!' they cried in wild chorus about him. 'To the Dance that never dies! To the sweet and fearful fantasy of evil!'

Another moment and he would have yielded and gone, for his will turned soft and the flood of passionate memory all but overwhelmed him, when—so can a small thing alter the whole course of an adventure—he caught his foot upon a loose stone in the edge of the wall, and then fell with a sudden crash on to the ground below. But he fell towards the houses, in the open space of dust and cobble stones, and fortunately not into the gaping depth of the valley on the farther side.

And they, too, came in a tumbling heap about him, like flies upon a piece of food, but as they fell he was released for a moment from the power of their touch, and in that brief instant of freedom there flashed into his mind the sudden intuition that saved him. Before he could regain his feet he saw them scrabbling awkwardly back upon the wall, as though bat-like they could only fly by dropping from a height, and had no hold upon him in the open. Then, seeing them perched there in a row like cats upon a roof, all dark and singularly shapeless, their eyes like lamps, the sudden memory came back to him of Ilsé's terror at the sight of fire.

Quick as a flash he found his matches and lit the dead leaves that lay under the wall.

Dry and withered, they caught fire at once, and the wind carried the flame in a long line down the length of the wall, licking upwards as it ran; and with shrieks and wailings, the crowded row of forms upon the top melted away into the air on the other side, and were gone with a great rush and whirring of their bodies down into the heart of the haunted valley, leaving Vezin breathless and shaken in the middle of the deserted ground.

'Ilsé!' he called feebly; 'Ilsé!' for his heart ached to think that she was really gone to the great Dance without him, and that he had lost the opportunity of its fearful joy. Yet at the same time his relief was so great, and he was so dazed and troubled in mind with the whole thing, that he hardly knew what he was saying, and only cried aloud in the fierce storm of his emotion. . . .

The fire under the wall ran its course, and the moonlight came out again, soft and clear, from its temporary eclipse. With one last shuddering look at the ruined ramparts, and a feeling of horrid wonder for the haunted valley beyond, where the shapes still crowded and flew, he turned his face towards the town and slowly made his way in the direction of the hotel.

And as he went, a great wailing of cries, and a sound of howling, followed him from the gleaming forest below, growing fainter and fainter with the bursts of wind as he disappeared between the houses.

* * *

'It may seem rather abrupt to you, this sudden tame ending,' said Arthur Vezin, glancing with flushed face and timid eyes at Dr. Silence sitting there with his notebook, 'but the fact is—er—from that moment my memory seems to have failed rather. I have no distinct recollection of how I got home or what precisely I did.

'It appears I never went back to the inn at all. I only dimly recollect racing down a long white road in the moonlight, past woods and villages, still and deserted, and then the dawn came up, and I saw the towers of a biggish town and so came to a station.

'But, long before that, I remember pausing somewhere on the road and looking back to where the hill-town of my adventure stood up in the moonlight, and thinking how exactly like a great monstrous cat it lay there upon the plain, its huge front paws lying down the two main streets, and the twin and broken towers of the cathedral marking its torn ears against the sky. That picture stays in my mind with the utmost vividness to this day.

'Another thing remains in my mind from that escape—namely, the sudden sharp reminder that I had not paid my bill, and the decision I made, standing there on the dusty highroad, that the small baggage I had left behind would more than settle for my indebtedness.

'For the rest, I can only tell you that I got coffee and bread at a café on the outskirts of this town I had come to, and soon after found my way to the station and caught a train later in the day. That same evening I reached London.'

'And how long altogether,' asked John Silence quietly, 'do you think you stayed in the town of the adventure?'

Vezin looked up sheepishly.

'I was coming to that,' he resumed, with apologetic wrigglings of his body. 'In London I found that I was a whole week out in my reckoning of time. I had stayed over a week in the town, and it ought to have been September 15th—instead of which it was only September 10th!'

'So that, in reality, you had only stayed a night or two in the inn?' queried the doctor.

Vezin hesitated before replying. He shuffled upon the mat.

'I must have gained time somewhere,' he said at length—'somewhere or somehow. I certainly had a week to my credit. I can't explain it. I can only give you the fact.'

'And this happened to you last year, since when you have never been back to the place?'

'Last autumn, yes,' murmured Vezin; 'and I have never dared to go back. I think I never want to.'

'And tell me,' asked Dr. Silence at length, when he saw that the little man had evidently come to the end of his words and had nothing more to say, 'had you ever read up the subject of the old witchcraft practices during the Middle Ages, or been at all interested in the subject?'

'Never!' declared Vezin emphatically. 'I had never given a thought to such matters so far as I know——'

'Or to the question of reincarnation, perhaps?'

'Never—before my adventure; but I have since,' he replied significantly.

There was, however, something still on the man's mind that

he wished to relieve himself of by confession, yet could with difficulty bring himself to mention; and it was only after the sympathetic tactfulness of the doctor had provided numerous openings that he at length availed himself of one of them, and stammered that he would like to show him the marks he still had on his neck where, he said, the girl had touched him with her anointed hands.

He took off his collar after infinite fumbling hesitation, and lowered his shirt a little for the doctor to see. And there, on the surface of the skin, lay a faint reddish line across the shoulder and extending a little way down the back towards the spine. It certainly indicated exactly the position an arm might have taken in the act of embracing. And on the other side of the neck, slightly higher up, was a similar mark, though not quite so clearly defined.

'That was where she held me that night on the ramparts,' he whispered, a strange light coming and going in his eyes.

It was some weeks later when I again found occasion to consult John Silence concerning another extraordinary case that had come under my notice, and we fell to discussing Vezin's story. Since hearing it, the doctor had made investigations on his own account, and one of his secretaries had discovered that Vezin's ancestors had actually lived for generations in the very town where the adventure came to him. Two of them, both women, had been tried and convicted as witches, and had been burned alive at the stake. Moreover, it had not been difficult to prove that the very inn where Vezin stayed was built about 1700 upon the spot where the funeral pyres stood and the executions took place. The town was a sort of headquarters for all the sorcerers and witches of the entire region, and after conviction they were burnt there literally by scores.

'It seems strange,' continued the doctor, 'that Vezin should have remained ignorant of all this; but, on the other hand, it was not the kind of history that successive generations would have been anxious to keep alive, or to repeat to their children. Therefore I am inclined to think he still knows nothing about it.

'The whole adventure seems to have been a very vivid revival of the memories of an earlier life, caused by coming directly into contact with the living forces still intense enough to hang about the place, and, by a most singular chance too, with the very souls who had taken part with him in the events of that particular life. For the mother and daughter who impressed him so strangely must have been leading actors, with himself, in the scenes and practices of witchcraft which at that period dominated the imaginations of the whole country.

'One has only to read the histories of the times to know that these witches claimed the power of transforming themselves into various animals, both for the purposes of disguise and also to convey themselves swiftly to the scenes of their imaginary orgies. Lycanthropy, or the power to change themselves into wolves, was everywhere believed in, and the ability to transform themselves into cats by rubbing their bodies with a special salve or ointment provided by Satan himself found equal credence. The witchcraft trials abound in evidences of such universal beliefs.'

Dr. Silence quoted chapter and verse from many writers on the subject, and showed how every detail of Vezin's had a basis in the practices of those dark days.

'But that the entire affair took place subjectively in the man's own consciousness, I have no doubt,' he went on, in reply to my questions; 'for my secretary who has been to the town to investigate, discovered his signature in the visitors' book, and proved by it that he had arrived on September 8th, and left suddenly without paying his bill. He left two days later, and they still were in possession of his dirty brown bag and some tourist clothes. I paid a few francs in settlement of his debt, and have sent his luggage on to him. The daughter was absent from home, but the proprietress, a large woman very much as he described her, told my secretary that he had seemed a very strange, absent-minded kind of gentleman, and after his disappearance she had feared for a long time that he had met with a violent end in the neighbouring forest where he used to roam about alone.

'I should like to have obtained a personal interview with the daughter so as to ascertain how much was subjective and how much actually took place with her as Vezin told it. For her dread of fire and the sight of burning must, of course, have been the intuitive memory of her former painful death at the stake, and have thus explained why he fancied more than once that he saw her through smoke and flame.'

'And that mark on his skin, for instance?' I inquired.

'Merely the marks produced by hysterical brooding,' he replied, 'like the stigmata of the *religieuses*, and the bruises which appear on the bodies of hypnotised subjects who have been told to expect them. This is very common and easily explained. Only it seems curious that these marks should have remained so long in Vezin's case. Usually they disappear quickly.'

'Obviously he is still thinking about it all, brooding, and living it all over again,' I ventured.

'Probably. And this makes me fear that the end of his trouble is not yet. We shall hear of him again. It is a case, alas! I can do little to alleviate.'

Dr. Silence spoke gravely and with sadness in his voice.

'And what do you make of the Frenchman in the train?' I asked further—'the man who warned him against the place, *à cause du sommeil et à cause des chats*? Surely a very singular incident?'

'A *very* singular incident indeed,' he made answer slowly, 'and one I can only explain on the basis of a highly improbable coincidence——'

'Namely?'

'That the man was one who had himself stayed in the town and undergone there a similar experience. I should like to find this man and ask him. But the crystal is useless here, for I have no slightest clue to go upon, and I can only conclude that some singular psychic affinity, some force still active in his being out of the same past life, drew him thus to the personality of Vezin, and enabled him to fear what might happen to him, and thus to warn him as he did.

'Yes,' he presently continued, half talking to himself, 'I suspect in this case that Vezin was swept into the vortex of forces arising out of the intense activities of a past life, and that he lived over again a scene in which he had often played a leading part centuries before. For strong actions set up forces that are so slow to exhaust themselves, they may be said in a sense never to die. In this case they were not vital enough to render the illusion complete, so that the little man found himself caught in a very distressing confusion of the present and the past; yet he was sufficiently sensitive to recognise that it was true, and to fight against the degradation of returning, even in memory, to a former and lower state of development.

'Ah yes!' he continued, crossing the floor to gaze at the darkening sky, and seemingly quite oblivious of my presence, 'subliminial up-rushes of memory like this can be exceedingly painful, and sometimes exceedingly dangerous. I only trust that this gentle soul may soon escape from this obsession of a passionate and tempestuous past. But I doubt it, I doubt it.'

His voice was hushed with sadness as he spoke, and when he turned back into the room again there was an expression of profound yearning upon his face, the yearning of a soul whose desire to help is sometimes greater than his power.

After the Black Magic stories of Dennis Wheatley—to which we shall come later—probably the other most famous series featuring Satanists and their activities are those which form the Cthulhu Mythos created by *H. P. Lovecraft*. This strange, retiring American who lived most of his life in obscurity and near-penury, is now one of the most revered names in the horror story genre and his tales a requisite inclusion for any popular macabre anthology. The Mythos was evolved through a series of stories and Lovecraft defined it himself as 'based on the fundamental lore or legend that this world was inhabited at one time by another race who, in practising black magic, lost their foothold and were expelled, yet live on outside ever ready to take possession of this earth again'. In these tales the earthly worshippers of the exiled Black Magicians constantly endeavour to find ways of bringing about their return. In 'The Festival'—which is one of the earliest stories written around the theme of the Mythos—Lovecraft demonstrates his great power at conjuring up atmosphere and also his ability to make the reader feel he is almost a part of the dreadful ritual in the night....

The Festival

H. P. LOVECRAFT

I was far from home, and the spell of the eastern sea was upon me. In the twilight I heard it pounding on the rocks, and I knew it lay just over the hill where the twisting willows writhed against the clearing sky and the first stars of evening. And because my fathers had called me to the old town beyond, I pushed on through the shallow, new-fallen snow along the road that soared lonely up to where Aldebaran twinkled among the trees; on toward the very ancient town I had never seen but often dreamed of.

It was the Yuletide, that men call Christmas though they know in their hearts it is older than Bethlehem and Babylon, older than Memphis and mankind. It was the Yuletide, and I had come at last to the ancient sea town where my people had dwelt and kept festival in the elder time when festival was forbidden; where also they had commanded their sons to keep festival once every century, that the memory of primal secrets might not be forgotten. Mine were an old people, and were old even when this land was settled three hundred years before. And they were strange, because they had come as dark furtive folk from opiate southern gardens of orchids, and spoken another tongue before they learnt the tongue of the blue-eyed fishers. And now they were scattered, and shared only the rituals of mysteries that none living could understand. I was the only one who came back that night to the old fishing town as legend bade, for only the poor and the lonely remember.

Then beyond the hill's crest I saw Kingsport outspread

frostily in the gloaming; snowy Kingsport with its ancient vanes and steeples, ridge-poles and chimney-pots, wharves and small bridges, willow-trees and graveyards; endless labyrinths of steep, narrow, crooked streets, and dizzy church-crowned central peak that time durst not touch; ceaseless mazes of colonial houses piled and scattered at all angles and levels like a child's disordered blocks; antiquity hovering on grey wings over winter-whitened gables and gambrel roofs; fanlights and small-paned windows one by one gleaming out in the cold dusk to join Orion and the archaic stars. And against the rotting wharves the sea pounded; the secretive, immemorial sea out of which the people had come in the elder time.

Beside the road at its crest a still higher summit rose, bleak and wind-swept, and I saw that it was a burying-ground where black gravestones stuck ghoulishly through the snow like the decayed fingernails of a gigantic corpse. The printless road was very lonely, and sometimes I thought I heard a distant horrible creaking as of a gibbet in the wind. They had hanged four kinsmen of mine for witchcraft in 1692, but I did not know just where.

As the road wound down the seaward slope I listened for the merry sounds of a village at evening, but did not hear them. Then I thought of the season, and felt that these old Puritan folk might well have Christmas customs strange to me, and full of silent hearthside prayer. So after that I did not listen for merriment or look for wayfarers, kept on down past the hushed lighted farmhouses and shadowy stone walls to where the signs of ancient shops and sea taverns creaked in the salt breeze, and the grotesque knockers of pillared doorways glistened along deserted unpaved lanes in the light of little, curtained windows.

I had seen maps of the town, and knew where to find the home of my people. It was told that I should be known and welcomed, for village legend lives long; so I hastened through Back Street to Circle Court, and across the fresh snow on the one full flagstone pavement in the town, to where Green Lane leads off behind the Market House. The old maps still held good, and I had no trouble; though at Arkham they must have lied when they said the trolleys ran to this place, since I saw not a wire overhead. Snow would have hid the rails in any case. I was glad I had chosen to walk, for the white village had seemed very beautiful from the hill; and now I was eager to knock at the door of my people, the seventh house on the left in Green Lane, with an ancient peaked roof and jutting second story, all built before 1650.

There were lights inside the house when I came upon it, and I saw from the diamond window-panes that it must have been kept very close to its antique state. The upper part overhung the narrow grass-grown street and nearly met the overhanging part of the house opposite, so that I was almost in a tunnel, with the low stone doorstep wholly free from snow. There was no sidewalk, but many houses had high doors reached by double flights of steps with iron railings. It was an odd scene, and because I was strange to New England I had never known its like before. Though it pleased me, I would have relished it better if there had been footprints in the snow, and people in the streets, and a few windows without drawn curtains.

When I sounded the archaic iron knocker I was half afraid. Some fear had been gathering in me, perhaps because of the strangeness of my heritage, and the bleakness of the evening, and the queerness of the silence in that aged town of curious customs. And when my knock was answered I was fully afraid, because I had not heard any footsteps before the door creaked open. But I was not afraid long, for the gowned, slippered old man in the doorway had a bland face that reassured me; and though he made signs that he was dumb, he wrote a quaint and ancient welcome with the stylus and wax tablet he carried.

He beckoned me into a low, candle-lit room with massive exposed rafters and dark, stiff, sparse furniture of the seventeenth century. The past was vivid there, for not an attribute was missing. There was a cavernous fireplace and a spinning-wheel at which a bent old woman in loose wrapper and deep poke-bonnet sat back toward me, silently spinning despite the festive season. An indefinite dampness seemed upon the place, and I marvelled that no fire should be blazing. The high-backed settle faced the row of curtained windows at the left, and seemed to be occupied, though I was not sure. I did not like everything about what I saw, and felt again the fear I had had. This fear grew stronger from what had before lessened it, for the more I looked at the old man's face the more its very blandness terrified me. The eyes never moved, and the skin was too much like wax. Finally I was sure it was not a face at all, but a fiendishly cunning mask. But the flabby hands, curiously gloved, wrote genially on the tablet and told me I must wait a while before I could be led to the place of the festival.

Pointing to a chair, table, and pile of books, the old man now left the room; and when I sat down to read I saw that the books were hoary and mouldy, and that they included old Morryster's wild *Marvells of Science*, the terrible *Saducismus Triumphatus* of Joseph Glanvil, published in 1681, the shocking *Daemonolatreia* of Remigius, printed in 1595 at Lyons, and worst of all, the unmentionable *Necronomicon* of the mad Arab Abdul Alhazred, in Olaus Wormius' forbidden Latin translation; a book which I had never seen, but of which I had heard monstrous things whispered. No one spoke to me, but I could hear the creaking of signs in the wind outside, and the whir of the wheel as the bonneted old woman continued her silent spinning, spinning. I thought the room and the books and the people very morbid and disquieting, but because an old tradition of my fathers had summoned me to strange feastings, I resolved to expect queer things. So I tried to read, and soon became tremblingly absorbed by something I found in that accursed *Necronomicon*; a thought and a legend too hideous for sanity or consciousness, but I disliked it when I fancied I heard the closing of one of the windows that the settle faced, as if it had been stealthily opened. It had seemed to follow a whirring that was not of the old woman's spinning-wheel. This was not much, though, for the old woman was spinning very hard, and the aged clock had been striking. After that I lost the feeling that there were persons on the settle, and was reading intently and shudderingly when the old man came back booted and dressed in a loose antique costume, and sat down on that very bench, so that I could not see him. It was certainly nervous waiting, and the blasphemous book in my hands made it doubly so. When eleven struck, however, the old man stood up, glided to a massive carved chest in a corner, and got two hooded cloaks; one of which he donned, and the other of which he draped round the old woman, who was ceasing her monotonous spinning. Then they both started for the outer door; the woman lamely creeping, and the old man, after picking up the very book I had been reading, beckoning me as he drew his hood over that unmoving face or mask.

We went out into the moonless and tortuous network of that incredibly ancient town; went out as the lights in the curtained windows disappeared one by one, and the Dog Star leered at the throng of cowled, cloaked figures that poured silently from every doorway and formed monstrous processions up this street and that, past the creaking signs and antediluvian gables, the thatched roofs and diamond-paned windows; threading precipitous lanes where decaying houses overlapped and crumbled together, gliding across open courts and churchyards where the bobbing lanthorns made eldritch drunken constellations.

Amid these hushed throngs I followed my voiceless guides; jostled by elbows that seemed preternaturally soft, and pressed by chests and stomachs that seemed abnormally pulpy; but seeing never a face and hearing never a word. Up, up, up, the eery columns slithered, and I saw that all the travellers were converging as they flowed near a sort of focus of crazy alleys at the top of a high hill in the centre of the town, where perched a great white church. I had seen it from the road's crest when I looked at Kingsport in the new dusk, and it had made me shiver because Aldebaran had seemed to balance itself a moment on the ghostly spire.

There was an open space around the church; partly a churchyard with spectral shafts, and partly a half-paved square swept nearly bare of snow by the wind, and lined with unwholesomely archaic houses having peaked roofs and overhanging gables. Death-fires danced over the tombs, revealing vistas, though queerly failing to cast any shadows. Past the churchyard, where there were no houses, I could see over the hill's summit and watch the glimmer of stars on the harbour, though the town was invisible in the dark. Only once in a while a lanthorn bobbed horribly through serpentine alleys on its way to overtake the throng that was now slipping speechlessly into the church. I waited till the crowd had oozed into the black doorway, and till all the stragglers had followed. The old man was pulling at my sleeve, but I was determined to be the last. Crossing the threshold into the swarming temple of unknown darkness, I turned once to look at the outside world as the churchyard phosphorescence cast a sickly glow on the hilltop pavement. And as I did so I shuddered. For though the wind had not left much snow, a few patches did remain on the path near the door; and in that fleeting backward look it seemed to my troubled eyes that they bore no mark of passing feet, nor even mine.

The church was scarce lighted by all the lanthorns that had entered it, for most of the throng had already vanished. They had streamed up the aisle between the high pews to the trapdoor of the vaults which yawned loathsomely open just before the pulpit, and were now squirming noiselessly in. I followed dumbly down the footworn steps and into the dark, suffocating crypt. The tail of that sinuous line of night-marchers seemed very horrible, and as I saw them wriggling into a venerable tomb they seemed more horrible still. Then I noticed that the tomb's floor had an aperture down which the throng was sliding, and in a moment we were all descending an ominous staircase of rough-hewn stone; a narrow spiral staircase damp and peculiarly odorous, that wound endlessly down into the bowels of the hill past monotonous walls of dripping stone blocks and crumbling mortar. It was a silent, shocking descent, and I observed after a horrible interval that the walls and steps were changing in nature, as if chiselled out of the solid rock. What mainly troubled me was that the myriad footfalls made no sound and set up no echoes. After more aeons of descent I saw some side passages or burrows leading from unknown recesses of blackness to this shaft of nighted mystery. Soon they became excessively numerous, like impious catacombs of nameless menace; and their pungent odour of decay grew quite unbearable. I knew we must have passed down through the mountain and beneath the earth of Kingsport itself, and I shivered that a town should be so aged and maggoty with subterraneous evil.

Then I saw the lurid shimmering of pale light, and heard the insidious lapping of sunless waters. Again I shivered, for I did not like the things that the night had brought, and wished bitterly that no forefather had summoned me to this primal rite. As the steps and the passage grew broader, I heard another sound, the thin, whining mockery of a feeble flute; and suddenly there spread out before me the boundless vista of an inner world—a vast fungous shore lit by a belching column of sick greenish flame and washed by a wide oily river that flowed from abysses frightful and unsuspected to join the blackest gulfs of immemorial ocean.

Fainting and gasping, I looked at that unhallowed Erebus of titan toadstools, leprous fire and slimy water, and saw the cloaked throngs forming a semicircle around the blazing pillar. It was the Yule-rite, older than man and fated to survive him; the primal rite of the solstice and of spring's promise beyond the snows; the rite of fire and evergreen, light and music. And in the stygian grotto I saw them do the rite, and adore the sick pillar of flame, and throw into the water handfuls gouged out of the viscous vegetation which glittered green in the chlorotic glare. I saw this, and I saw something amorphously squatted far away from the light, piping noisomely on a flute; and as the thing piped I thought I heard noxious muffled flutterings in the foetid darkness where I could not see. But what frightened me most was that flaming column; spouting volcanically from depths profound and inconceivable, casting no shadows as healthy flame should, and coating the nitrous stone with a nasty, venomous verdigris. For in all that seething combustion no warmth lay, but only the clamminess of death and corruption.

The man who had brought me now squirmed to a point directly beside the hideous flame, and made stiff ceremonial motions to the semicircle he faced. At certain stages of the ritual they did grovelling obeisance, especially when he held above his head that abhorrent *Necronomicon* he had taken with him; and I shared all the obeisances because I had been summoned to this festival by the writings of my forefathers. Then the old man made a signal to the half-seen flute-player in the darkness, which player thereupon changed its feeble drone to a scarce louder drone in another key; precipitating as it did so a horror unthinkable and unexpected. At this horror I sank nearly to the lichened earth, transfixed with a dread not of this or any world, but only of the mad spaces between the stars.

Out of the unimaginable blackness beyond the gangrenous glare of that cold flame, out of the tartarean leagues through which that oily river rolled uncanny, unheard, and unsuspected, there flopped rhythmically a horde of tame, trained, hybrid winged things that no sound eye could ever wholly grasp, or sound brain ever wholly remember. They were not altogether crows, nor moles, nor buzzards, nor ants, nor vampire bats, nor decomposed human beings; but something I cannot and must not recall. They flopped limply along, half with their webbed feet and half with their membranous wings; and as they reached the throng of celebrants the cowled figures seized and mounted them, and rode off one by one along the reaches of that unlighted river, into pits and galleries of panic where poison springs feed frightful cataracts.

The old spinning woman had gone with the throng, and the old man remained only because I had refused when he motioned me to seize an animal and ride like the rest. I saw when I staggered to my feet that the amorphous flute-player had rolled out of sight, but that two of the beasts were patiently standing by. As I hung back, the old man produced his stylus and tablet and wrote that he was the true deputy of my fathers who had founded the Yule worship in this ancient place; that it had been decreed I should come back, and that the most secret mysteries were yet to be performed. He wrote this in a very ancient hand, and when I still hesitated he pulled from his loose robe a seal ring and a watch, both with my family arms, to prove that he was what he said. But it was a hideous proof, because I knew from old papers that that watch had been buried with my great-great-great-great-grandfather in 1698.

Presently the old man drew back his hood and pointed to the family resemblance in his face, but I only shuddered, because I was sure that the face was merely a devilish waxen mask. The flopping animals were now scratching restlessly at the lichens, and I saw that the old man was nearly as restless himself. When one of the things began to waddle and edge away, he turned quickly to stop it; so that the suddenness of his motion dislodged the waxen mask from what should have been his head. And then, because that nightmare's position barred me from the stone staircase down which we had come, I flung myself into the oily underground river that bubbled somewhere to the caves of the sea; flung myself into that putrescent juice of earth's inner horrors before the madness of my screams could bring down upon me all the charnel legions these pest-gulfs might conceal . . .

At the hospital they told me I had been found half-frozen in Kingsport Harbour at dawn, clinging to the drifting spar that accident sent to save me. They told me I had taken the wrong fork of the hill road the night before, and fallen over the cliffs at Orange Point; a thing they deduced from prints found in the snow. There was nothing I could say, because everything was wrong. Everything was wrong, with the broad windows showing a sea of roofs in which only about one in five was ancient, and the sound of trolleys and motors in the streets below. They insisted that this was Kingsport, and I could not deny it. When I went delirious at hearing that the hospital stood near the old churchyard on Central Hill, they sent me to St. Mary's Hospital in Arkham, where I could have better care. I liked it there, for the doctors were broad-minded, and even lent me their influence in obtaining the carefully sheltered copy of Alhazred's objectionable *Necronomicon* from the library of Miskatonic University. They said something about a 'psychosis', and agreed I had better get any harassing obsessions off my mind.

So I read that hideous chapter, and shuddered doubly because it was indeed not new to me. I had seen it before, let footprints tell what they might; and where it was I had seen it were best forgotten. There was no one—in waking hours—who could remind me of it; but my dreams are filled with terror, because of phrases I dare not quote. I dare quote only one paragraph, put into such English as I can make from the awkward Low Latin.

'The nethermost caverns,' wrote the mad Arab, 'are not for the fathoming of eyes that see; for their marvels are strange and terrific. Cursed the ground where dead thoughts live new and oddly bodied, and evil the mind that is held by no head. Wisely did Ibn Schacabao say, that happy is the tomb where no wizard hath lain, and happy the town at night whose wizards are all ashes. For it is of old rumour that the soul of the devil-bought hastes not from his charnel clay, but fats and instructs *the very worm that gnaw*; till out of corruption horrid life springs, and the dull scavengers of earth wax crafty to vex it and swell monstrous to plague it. Great holes secretly are digged where earth's pores ought to suffice, and things have learnt to walk that ought to crawl.'

Since his death, a number of admirers of H. P. Lovecraft have not only worked successfully to bring his name to international recognition, but have also created stories along the lines of the Cthulhu Mythos. Of all these men, *August Derleth*, himself a writer of weird tales and a distinguished anthologist, is probably the most famous. Derleth, through his publishing company Arkham House, has been mainly responsible for collecting and issuing the products of Lovecraft's pen and also for examining and explaining the older man's work. This has not surprisingly given him a splendid inside knowledge of Lovecraft's various designs and enabled him to write new stories in the same vein and carrying the same developments still further. The story which follows, 'The Watcher From The Sky', is in my opinion quite the best in the new series and the one which is most complete in itself and therefore understandable to the reader encountering the Mythos for the first time. This marks the first publication of the story outside America—I hope it will not be long before there are others.

The Watcher from the Sky

AUGUST DERLETH

'Abel Keane . . . Abel Keane . . . Abel Keane. . . .'

Sometimes I am constrained to speak my name aloud, as if to reassure myself that all is as before, that indeed I am Abel Keane; and I find myself walking to the mirror and looking at myself, scrutinising the familiar lineaments for any sign of change. As if there must be change! As if surely, some time, change must come, the change that marks the experiences of that week. Or was it but a week? Or less? I do not any longer have assurance of anything.

It is a terrible thing to lose faith in the world of daylight and the night of stars, to feel that at any time all the known laws of space and time may be abrogated, may be thrust aside as by some sorcery, by ancient evil known only to a few men, whose voices are indeed voices crying in the wilderness.

I have hesitated until now to tell what I know of the fire which destroyed a great portion of a certain seaport town on the Massachusetts coast, of the abomination which existed there, but events have dictated that I hesitate no longer. There are things men should not know, and it is always difficult for any one man to decide whether to make certain facts known, or to hold them in abeyance. There was a reason for the fire—a reason known only to two people, though surely there were others who suspected—but not outside that shunned town. It has been said that if any man had a vision of the incredible vastnesses of outer space and the knowledge of what exists there, that alone would drive him stark, raving mad. But there are things that go on within the boundaries of our own small earth which are no less frightening, things that bind us to the entire cosmos, to colossi of time and space, to evil and horror so old, so ancient that the entire history of mankind is but a vapour in the air beside them.

Of such was the reason for that destructive fire, that fire which destroyed far more than it was meant to destroy, block after block of that loathed town across to the Manuxet on the one side and to the shore of the sea on another. They called it arson—but only for a little while. They found some of those little stones—but there was nothing but one mention in the papers of either arson or those peculiar stone pieces. The townspeople saw to that; they were quick to suppress it; their own fire examiners put out an entirely different story. They said that the man who was lost in the fire had fallen asleep beside his lamp and had knocked it over, and that that was the way the fire started. . . .

But it was arson, technically speaking—justifiable arson. . . .

* * *

Evil is the special province, surely, of the student of divinity.

Such was I on that Summer night when I unlocked the door of my room at my lodging house, Number 17, Thoreau Drive, in the city of Boston, Massachusetts—and found lying on my bed a strange man, clad in alien garments, lying in a deep sleep from which I could not at first awaken him. Since my door was locked, he must have entered by way of the open window—but of how he had come, by what incredible passage, I was not immediately to know.

After my initial surprise had passed, I examined my visitor. He was a young man of approximately thirty years of age; he was clean-shaven, dark-skinned, and lithe; he was clothed in loose-flowing robes of a material foreign to me, and he wore sandals made from the leather of some beast whose identity was unknown to me. Though it was evident that he carried various articles in the pockets of that strange clothing, I did not examine them. He was in a sleep so deep that it was impossible to awaken him, and evidence showed that he had virtually fallen across the bed and had gone instantly to sleep.

I discovered at once that there was something familiar about his features—familiar with that strange insistence so commonly associated with people whom one has known before, perhaps casually, but nevertheless has known. Either I had my visitor's acquaintance, or I had seen his picture somewhere. It occurred to me at this point that I might well attempt to learn his identity while he slept, and accordingly I drew a chair up to the bed and sat down beside my visitor, intending to practise auto-suggestion, which I had learned from indulgence in my lesser professional existence—for, while working my way through divinity school, I appeared thrice weekly on public and occasionally on private stages as an amateur hypnotist, and some small study of the human mind had enabled me to accomplish various trivial successes in mind-reading and allied matters.

However, deep as his sleep was, he was *aware*.

I cannot explain this even now, but it was as if, though his body slept, his senses did not, for he spoke as I leaned above him, motivated by my intention; and he spoke out of a patent awareness which must be related to his strange way of life about which I learned later, a development from a super-sensory existence.

'Wait,' he said. And then, 'Be patient, Abel Keane.'

And suddenly a most curious reaction was manifest within myself; it felt precisely as if someone or something had invaded me, as if my visitor spoke to me without words to tell me his name, for his lips did not appear to move, yet I was distinctly aware of the impression of words. 'I am Andrew Phelan. I left this room two years ago; I have come back for a little while.' Thus directly, thus simply, I knew; and I knew too that I had seen Andrew Phelan's likeness in the Boston papers at the time of his utterly outré disappearance from this very room two years previously, a disappearance never satisfactorily explained.

Excitement possessed me.

So strong was my impression of his *awareness*, despite his aspect of sleep, that I could not forebear asking him, 'Where have you been?'

'Celaeno,' came his prompt reply, but whether he actually spoke, or whether he merely communicated it to me without words, I cannot now say.

And where was Celaeno? I wondered.

He woke at two o'clock in the morning. Tired myself, I had fallen into a light slumber, from which I was awakened by his hand on my shoulder. I was startled and gazed up to find his firm eyes looking steadily and appraisingly at me. He was still clad in his curious robe, but his first thought was for clothing.

'Have you an extra suit?'

'Yes.'

'I shall need to borrow it. We are not unlike in build, and I cannot go out like this. Will you mind?'

'No—by all means.'

'I am sorry to have deprived you of your bed, but my long journey tired me very much.'

'If I may ask, how did you get in?'

He gestured to the window.

'Why here?'

'Because this room was my point of contact,' he answered enigmatically. He then looked at his watch. 'The suit now, if you don't mind. My time is short.'

I felt impelled to get the clothing he wished, and did so. When he disrobed, I saw that he was very strong, very muscular, and he moved with an agility that made me doubt my first guess as to his age. I said nothing as he dressed; he remarked casually on the good fit of the suit, which was not my best, though it was neat and clean and had just been pressed. I told him equally as casually that he was welcome to it for as long as he needed it.

'The landlady is still Mrs. Brier?' he asked then.

'Yes.'

'I hope you will say nothing to her of me; it would only trouble her.'

'To no one?'

'No one.'

He began to move to the door, and instantly I apprehended that he meant to be gone. At the same time I was aware of not wanting him to leave without imparting to me more information about the mystery which had remained unsolved for two years. Rashly, I sprang up and threw myself between him and the door.

He looked at me with calm, amused eyes.

'Wait!' I cried. 'You can't go like this! What is it you want? Let me get it for you.'

He smiled. 'I seek evil, Mr. Keane—evil that is more terrible than anything taught in your school of divinity, believe me.'

'Evil is my field, Mr. Phelan.'

'I guarantee nothing,' he replied. 'The risks are too great for ordinary men.'

An insane impulse took possession of me. I was seized with the urgent desire to accompany my visitor, even if it became necessary to hypnotise him. I fixed his strange eyes with mine, I reached out my hands—and then something happened to me. I found myself suddenly on another plane, in another dimension, as it were. I felt that I had taken Andrew Phelan's place on the bed, and yet accompanied him in spirit. For instantly, soundlessly, painlessly, I was out of this world. Nothing else would describe the sensations I experienced for the remainder of that night.

I saw, I heard, I felt and tasted and smelled things utterly alien to my consciousness. He did not touch me; he only looked at me. Yet I apprehended instantly that I stood on the edge of an abyss of horror unimaginable! Whether he led me to the bed or whether I made my own way there I do not know; yet it was on the bed that I found myself in the morning after those memorable hours of the remainder of that night. Did I sleep and dream? Or did I lie in hypnosis and know because Phelan willed me to know all that took place? It was better for my sanity to believe that I dreamed.

And what dreams! What magnificent and yet terror-fraught images wrought by the sub-conscious! And Andrew Phelan was everywhere in those dreams. I saw him in that darkness making his way to a bus station, taking a bus; I saw him in the bus, as if I sat beside him; I saw him alight at ancient, legend-haunted and shunned Innsmouth, after changing buses at Arkham. I was beside him when he prowled down along that wrecked waterfront with its sinister ruins—and I saw where he paused, before that disguised refinery, and later at that one-time Masonic hall which now bore over its doorway the curious legend: *Esoteric Order of Dagon.* And yet more—I witnessed the beginning of that strange pursuit, when the first of those hideous batrachian men emerged from the shadows along the Manuxet River and took up the trail of Andrew Phelan, the uncanny silent followers after the seeker of evil, until Phelan turned his steps away from Innsmouth. . . .

All night long, hour after hour, until the sun rose, and dream and actuality became one, and I opened my eyes to look at Andrew Phelan entering my room. I pulled myself together, smiling sheepishly, and swung to the edge of the bed, where I sat looking at him.

'I think you owe me an explanation,' I said.

'It is better not to know too much,' he answered.

'One cannot fight evil without knowledge,' I retorted.

He said nothing in reply, but I pressed him. He sat down somewhat wearily. Did he not think that some explanation ought to be given me? I demanded. He then countered with an enigmatic suggestion that there were certain age-old horrors which were better left unrevealed; this only excited my curiosity the more. Did it not occur to me, he wanted to know, that there might be certain dislocations in space and time infinitely more terrible than any known horror? Had I never thought that there might be other planes, other dimensions beyond the known planes and dimensions? Had I not considered that space might exist in conterminous folds, that time might be a dimension capable of being travelled backward as well as forward? He spoke to me thus in riddles, and carried on in this fashion despite all my attempts to question him.

'I am only trying to protect you, Keane,' he said finally, still with infinite patience.

'Did you escape your pursuer in Innsmouth last night?'

He nodded.

'You knew of him, then?'

'Yes, or you would not have been aware of him, for in your —shall we say, hypnosis?—you could know only such things of which I was cognizant. I suggest to you, Keane, that hypnotism is a dangerous means; I thought it might serve as a warning if it were turned back upon you last night.'

'That was not alone hypnotism.'

'Perhaps not as you know it.' He made a gesture of dismissal. 'Would it be possible for me to rest here for a while today before pursuing my quest? I would not like to be discovered by Mrs. Brier.'

'I'll see to it that you're not disturbed.'

Even as I spoke, I had made up my mind what to do; I was determined that Andrew Phelan would not put me off so easily, and there was one course left open to me—I could discover certain things for myself. Despite his caution, my visitor had dropped hints and suggestions. Even beyond them, however, there was the mystery of Andrew Phelan itself; that had been extensively recorded in the daily papers of that time; certainly in those accounts I might expect to discover some clue. I adjured Phelan to make himself comfortable, and departed, ostensibly for the college; but instead, once outside, I telephoned to excuse myself from that day's study. Then, after a light breakfast, I took myself off to the Widener Library in Cambridge.

Andrew Phelan had said that he had come from Celaeno. This hint was too patent for me to overlook; so forthwith I set myself to track down Celaeno. I found it sooner than I had expected to find it—but it solved nothing. If anything, it served only to deepen the mystery of Andrew Phelan.

For Celaeno was one of the stars in the Pleiades cluster of Taurus!

I turned next to the files of the newspapers concerning Phelan's vanishing, early in September, 1938. I hoped to discover in the accounts of this remarkable disappearance without trace from out the window of that same room to which he had now returned, something to lead me to some feasible explanation. But as I read the accounts, my perplexity deepened; there was a singularly complete puzzlement expressed in the newspapers. But there were certain dark hints, certain vague and ominous suggestions which fastened to my awareness. Phelan had been employed by Dr. Laban Shrewsbury of Arkham. Like Phelan, Dr. Shrewsbury had spent some years in a strange and never-explained absence from his home, to which he had returned as queerly as now Andrew Phelan had come back. Shortly before Phelan's disappearance, Dr. Shrewsbury's house, together with the doctor himself, had been destroyed by fire. Phelan's tasks had apparently been secretarial, but he had spent a good deal of his time in the Library of Miskatonic University in Arkham.

So it seemed to me that the only definite clue offered to me at the Widener was in Arkham; for the records of the Miskatonic University Library should certainly reveal what books Phelan had consulted—presumably in the interests of the late Dr. Shrewsbury. Only an hour had now elapsed; there was ample time for me to pursue my search; so forthwith I took a bus out of Boston for Arkham, and, in a comparatively short time, I was put down not far from the institution within the walls of which I believed I would discover some further information about Andrew Phelan's pursuits.

My inquiry about the records of books used by Andrew Phelan was met with a curious kind of reticence, and resulted in my being shown ultimately into the office of the director of the library, Dr. Llanfer, who wished to know why I sought to consult certain books always kept under lock and key by the express order of the library's directors. I explained that I had become interested in the disappearance of Andrew Phelan, and in the work he had been doing.

His eyes narrowed. 'Are you a reporter?'

'I am a student, sir.' Fortunately, I had with me my college credentials, and lost no time in showing them to him.

'Very well.' He nodded and, however reluctantly, wrote out the desired permission on a slip of paper and handed it to me. 'It is only fair to tell you, Mr. Keane, that of the several people who have consulted these books at length, few—if any—are alive to tell about it.'

On this singularly sinister note I was shown out of his office, and presently found myself being conveyed to a little room that was hardly more than a cubicle, where I sat down while the attendant assigned to me placed before me certain books and papers. Chief among them, and obviously the most prized possession of the library, judging by the almost reverent way in which the attendant handled it, was an ancient volume entitled simply *Necronomicon*, by an Arab, Abdul Alhazred. The records showed that Phelan had consulted this volume on several occasions, but, much to my chagrin, it was clear that this volume was not for the uninitiate, for it contained references which for ambiguity were unexcelled. But of one thing I could be certain—the book pertained to evil and horror, to terror and fear of the unknown, to things that walk in the night, and not alone the little night of man, but that vaster, deeper, more mysterious night of the world—the dark side of existence.

I turned from this book in near despair, and found myself looking into a manuscript copy of a book by Professor Shrewsbury: *Cthulhu in the Necronomicon*. And in these pages, quite by accident—for this book, too, consisted of learned and scholarly paragraphs concerning the lore of the Arab, most of them utterly beyond my comprehension—I came upon a certain reference which imparted to me, in the light of what small experience I had already had, a frightening chill and a feeling of the utmost dread. For, as I scanned the pages with their enigmatic allusions to beings and places utterly alien to me, I found in the midst of a quotation purporting to be from another book entitled the *R'lyeh Text*, the following: '*Great Cthulhu shall rise from R'lyeh, Hastur the Unspeakable shall return from the dark star which is in the Hyades near Aldebaran ... Nyarlathotep shall howl forever in the darkness where he abideth, Shub-Niggurath shall spawn his thousand young ...*'

I read—and read again. It was incredible, damnable—but for the second time within twenty-four hours, I had come upon reference to unbelievable spaces, and to stars—to a star in the Hyades, a star in Taurus—and surely it could be none other than Celaeno!

And, as if in mocking answer to the question which loomed so large before me, I turned over this manuscript, and found below it a portfolio labelled in a strong, if spidery hand: *Celaeno Fragments!* I drew it toward me, and found it sealed. At this, the aged attendant, who had been observing me closely, came over.

'It has never been opened,' he said.

'Not even by Mr. Phelan?'

He shook his head. 'Since it came by Mr. Phelan's hand, with Dr. Shrewsbury's seal on it, we do not believe he had access to it. We do not know.'

I looked at my watch. Time was passing now, and I meant to go on to Innsmouth before I completed my day. Reluctantly, and yet with a strange sense of foreboding, I pushed away the manuscripts and books.

'I will come again,' I promised. 'I want to get to Innsmouth before too much of the day has gone.'

The attendant favoured me with a curious and reflective gaze. 'Yes, it is better to visit Innsmouth by day,' he said finally.

I pondered this while the old man gathered up the papers and books. Then I said, 'That is surely a curious statement to make, Mr. Peabody. Is there anything wrong with Innsmouth?'

'Ah, do not ask me. *I* have never gone there. I have no desire to go there. There are strange things enough in Arkham, without the need for going on to Innsmouth. But I have heard things—terrible things, Mr. Keane, such things that it may well be said of them that it is of no account whatever whether or not they are true, but of account only that they are being said. What they do say of the Marshes, who have the refinery there . . .'

'Refinery!' I cried, remembering my dream.

'Yes. It was old Obed Marsh first, old Captain Obed—they said—well, what does it matter? He is gone, and now it is Ahab who is there, Ahab Marsh—his great-grandson—and he is no longer young. But he is not old, either; they do not get very old in Innsmouth.'

'What did they say of Obed Marsh?'

'It does not matter to tell it, I suppose. Perhaps it is an old wives' tale—that he was leagued with the devil and brought a great plague to Innsmouth in 1846, and that those who came after him were bound by compacts with unearthly beings from beyond that Devil Reef off Innsmouth Harbour, and brought about the destruction by dynamite of many old houses and the wharves along the seashore there during the winter of 'twenty-seven and 'eight. There are not many living there, and no one likes the Innsmouth people.'

'Race prejudice?'

'It is something about them—they do not seem like people—that is, people like the rest of us. I saw one of them once—he made me think—you may think it an old men's aberration, but I assure you it is not; he made me think of a frog!'

I was shaken. The creature who had so shadowily crept after Andrew Phelan in my dream or vision of the night before had seemed bestially frog-like. I was at the same time possessed of the urgent desire to go to Innsmouth and see for myself the places of my dream-haunted repose.

Yet when I stood before Hammond's Drug Store in Market Square, waiting for the ancient and shunned bus which carried venturesome travellers to Innsmouth and went on to Newburyport, I had a sense of impending danger so strong that I could not shake it off. Despite my insistent curiosity, I was sharply, keenly aware of a kind of sixth sense prompting me not to take the bus driven by that queer, sullen-visaged fellow, who brought the bus to a stop and came out to walk briefly, suggestively stooped, into Hammond's before setting forth on the journey to Innsmouth, the final object of my somewhat aimless search that day.

I did not yield to that prompting, but climbed into the bus, which I shared with but one other passenger, whom I knew instinctively to be an Innsmouth resident, for he, too, had a strange cast of features, with odd, deep creases in the sides of his neck, a narrow-headed fellow who could not have been more than forty, with the bulging, watery blue eyes and flat nose and curiously undeveloped ears which I was to find so shockingly common in that shunned seaport town toward which the bus soon began to roll. The driver, too, was manifestly an Innsmouth man, and I began to understand what Mr. Peabody had meant when he spoke of the Innsmouth people as seeming somehow 'not like people'. To the end of comparison with that following figure of my dream, I scrutinised both my fellow-passenger and the driver as closely, if furtively, as I could; and I was somewhat relieved to come to the conclusion that there was a subtle difference. I could not put my finger on it, but the follower of my dream seemed malign, in contrast to these people, who had merely that appearance so common to cretins and similar unfortunate individuals bearing the stigmata of lower intelligence in the realm of the subnormal more especially than that of the abnormal.

I had never before been to Innsmouth. Having come down from New Hampshire to pursue my divinity studies, I had had no occasion to travel beyond Arkham. Therefore, the town as I saw it as the bus approached it down the slope of the coast-line there, had a most depressing effect on me, for it was strangely dense, and yet seemed devoid of life. No cars drove out to pass us coming in, and of the three steeples rising above the chimney-pots and the crouching gambrel roofs and peaked gables, many of them sagging with decay, only one had any semblance whatsoever of use, for the others were weather-beaten, with gaps in them where shingles had been torn away, and badly needed paint. For that matter, the entire town seemed to need paint—all, that is, save two buildings we passed, the two buildings of my dream, the refinery and that imposing, pillared hall standing among the churches which clustered about the radial point of the town's streets, with its black and gold sign on the pediment, so vividly remembered from my experience of the previous night—the *Esoteric Order of Dagon.* This structure, like that of the Marsh Refining Company along the Manuxet River, seemed to have been given a coat of paint only recently. Apart from this, and a single store of the First National chain, all the buildings in what was apparently the business district of the town were repellently old, with paint peeling from them, and their windows badly in need of washing. It was so, too, of the town generally, though the old residential streets of Broad, Washington, Lafayette, and Adams, where lived still those who were left of Innsmouth's old families—the Marshes, the Gilmans, the Eliots, and the Waites—were of a fresher appearance, not so much in obvious need of paint as of refurbishing, for the grounds grew wild and rank, and in many cases, fences—now overgrown with vines—had been constructed to make the casual view of passers-by different.

Repelled as I was by the Innsmouth people, I stood for a few moments on the curb, after having left the bus and ascertained the hour when it would return to Arkham—at seven that evening—wondering just what course it would be best to follow. I had no desire to speak to the people of Innsmouth, for I had the strongest of forebodings that to do so was to court subtle and insidious danger; yet I continued to be impelled by the curiosity which had brought me here. It occurred to me, as I stood pondering, that the manager of the First National chain store might very well not be one of the Innsmouth people; it was the custom of the chain to move its managers around, and there was just a chance that the man in charge of this store was an outsider—for among these people, it was inevitable that anyone from beyond the immediate vicinity would be made to feel tangibly that he was an outsider. Accordingly, I made my way over to the corner where the store stood, and entered it.

Contrary to my expectations, there were no clerks, but only a man of middle age, who was at work on a prosaic display of canned goods as I entered and asked for the manager. But clearly, he was the manager; he did not bear any of those oddly shocking distinguishing marks so common to the people of Innsmouth; so he was, as I had guessed, an outsider. I observed with a faint sense of unpleasant distaste that he was startled to look at me, and seemed hesitant to speak, but I realised immediately that this was no doubt due to his isolation among these curiously decayed people.

Having introduced myself, and observed aloud that I could recognise him for an outsider, like myself, I at once pursued my inquiry. What was it about these Innsmouth people? I wanted to know. What was the *Esoteric Order of Dagon*? And what was being said about Ahab Marsh?

His reaction was instantaneous. Nor was it entirely unexpected. He became agitated, he glanced fearfully toward the entrance to the store, and then came over to seize me almost roughly by the arm.

'We don't talk about such things here,' he said in a harsh whisper.

His nervous fear was only too manifest.

'I'm sorry if I distressed you,' I went on, 'but I'm only a casual traveller and I'm curious as to why such a potentially fine port should be all but abandoned. Indeed, it is virtually abandoned; the wharves have not been repaired, and many business places seem closed.'

He shuddered. 'Do *they* know you are asking questions?'

'You are the first person to whom I have spoken.'

'Thank God! Take my advice and leave town as soon as you can. You can take a bus . . .'

'I came in on the bus. I want to know something about the town.'

He looked at me indecisively, glanced once more toward the entrance, and then, turning abruptly and walking along a counter toward a curtained door which apparently shut off his own quarters, he said, 'Come along with me, Mr. Keane.'

In his own rooms at the rear of the store, he began, however reluctantly, to talk in harsh whispers, as if he feared the very walls might hear. What I wanted to know, he said, was impossible to tell, because there was no *proof* of it. All was talk, talk and the terrible decay of isolated families, intermarrying generation after generation. That accounted in part for what he called 'the Innsmouth look'. It was true, old Captain Obed Marsh held commerce with the far corners of the earth, and he brought strange things—and some said, strange practices like that seafarers' kind of pagan worship called the *Esoteric Order of Dagon*—back to Innsmouth with him. It was said that he held stranger commerce with creatures that rose in the dark of the moon out of the deep sea beyond Devil Reef and met him at the reef, a mile and a half out from shore, but he knew of no one who had seen them, though it was said that in the winter of the year when the Federal government had destroyed the waterfront buildings, a submarine had gone out and discharged torpedoes *straight down* into the unfathomable depths beyond Devil Reef. He spoke persuasively and well; perhaps indeed he knew no more, but I felt undeniably the lacunae in his story—the unanswered questions being inherent in all that he said.

There were stories about Captain Obed Marsh, yes. Because

of them, there were stories about all the Marshes. But there were stories about the Waites, the Gilmans, the Ornes, and the Eliots, too—about all the old, one-time wealthy families. And it was true that it was not wise to linger in the vicinity of the Marsh Refining Company building, or near the Order of Dagon Hall. . . .

At this point our conversation was interrupted by the tinkling of the bell announcing a customer, and Mr. Hendreson immediately left to answer the summons. I peered curiously from between the folds of the curtain and saw that a woman had come in—an Innsmouth woman, for her appearance was instantly chilling and repulsive; there was something more than just similarity to the men about her, there was a kind of almost reptilian menace, and she spoke in a thick mutation of speech, though Hendreson seemed to understand it all right and waited on her without comment of any kind, save to answer her questions with an air that was rather more than just civil, rather subservient.

'That was one of the Waite women,' he said in answer to my question when he returned. 'They're all like that—and the Marsh women were before them. The Marshes are all gone now, all except Ahab and the two old women.'

'The refinery still runs, then?'

'A little. The Marshes still have some ships; there was a long time after the government was here when they had nothing at all in the way of ships; then in the middle thirties they bought a few again, this Ahab came up from nobody knows where, just came in on a ship one night, they say, and took over where the Marshes left off. Cousin or great-grandson, they say. Saw him once, and that at a distance. Doesn't go out much—except to the Hall—the Marshes always did sort of run that show.'

The *Esoteric Order of Dagon*, he explained in response to my insistent prying, was a kind of ancient worship, pagan certainly, and outsiders were rigidly excluded from any knowledge of it. It was not healthy even to ask about it. My schooling rebelled at this, and I demanded to know what part the ministers of the other churches were playing in this? To this he responded with a further question: why not ask denominational headquarters for this district? I would discover that the various denominations disowned their own churches, and the pastors of those churches had sometimes simply disappeared, and at other times had undergone strange reversions to primitive and pagan ceremonies in their worship.

Everything he said was disturbing far beyond anything within the limits of my experience. And yet, what he said was not nearly so terrifying as what remained only implied in his words—the vague hints of terrifying evil, of evil from *outside*, the hideous suggestiveness of what had taken place between the Marshes and those creatures from the deep, the lurking unvoiced assumption of what went on at the meetings of the *Esoteric Order of Dagon*. Something had happened here in 1928, something terrible enough to be kept out of the press, something to bring the Federal government down to the scene and to justify the havoc wrought along the ocean's edge in the wharf district of this old fishing town. I knew enough Biblical history to know that Dagon was the ancient fish-like god of the Philistines, who rose from the waters of the Red Sea, but there was ever present in my thoughts the belief that the Dagon of Innsmouth was but a fictive mask of that earlier pagan God, that the Dagon of Innsmouth was the symbol of something noxious and infinitely terrible, something that might account not only for the curious aspect of the Innsmouth people, but also for the fact that Innsmouth was shunned and forsaken, let alone by the rest of the towns in its vicinity, and forgotten by the outside world.

I pressed the storekeeper for something definite, but he could not or would not give it; indeed, he began to act, as time wore on, as if I had already been told far too much, his agitation increased, and presently I thought it best to take my leave, though Hendreson implored me not to carry on any overt investigation, saying at the last that people had been known to 'drop out of sight, and the Lord alone knows where. Nobody ever found a clue as to where they went, and I reckon nobody ever will. But *they* know.'

On this sinister note I took my leave.

Time did not permit much further exploration, but I managed to walk about a few of the streets and lanes of Innsmouth near the bus station, and found everything in a state of curious decay, and most of the buildings giving off besides that familiar odour of old wood and stone, a strange watery essence as of the sea. Farther I could not go, for I was disturbed by the queer glances given me by the few inhabitants I passed on the streets, and I was ever conscious of being under surveillance from behind closed doors and window curtains; but most of all, I was horribly aware of a kind of aura of malevolence, so keenly aware of it indeed that I was glad when at last the time came for me to take the bus and make my way back to Arkham and thence to my room in Boston.

* * *

Andrew Phelan was waiting for me when I returned.

The night was almost half gone, but Phelan had not left my room. I thought he looked at me a little pityingly when I entered.

'I have often wondered why it is that human curiosity is insatiable,' he said, 'but I suppose it is too much to expect that one who has had an experience like yours, so far from the norm of things as most of us know it, should accept it without seeking explanation other than that I gave you.'

'You know?'

'Where you have been? Yes. Did anyone follow you, Abel?'

'I didn't look to see.'

He shook his head mutely. 'And did you learn what you sought to learn?'

I confessed that I was more puzzled than ever. And, yes, a little more disturbed than I had been at first. 'Celaeno,' I said. 'What have you been telling me?'

'We are both there,' he said bluntly, 'Dr. Shrewsbury and I.'

For a moment I thought he was resorting to bluff; but there was something in his attitude that forbade levity. He was grim, unsmiling.

'You think that is impossible? You are bound by your own laws. Do not think further of it, but simply accept what I say for the time being. For years Dr. Shrewsbury and I have been on the trail of a great evil being, determined to close the avenues by which he may return to terrestrial life out of his enchanted prison beneath the sea. Listen to me, Abel, and understand in what deadly peril you stood this afternoon in accursed Innsmouth.'

Thereupon he launched into a soul-shaking account of incredible, ancient evil, of Great Old Ones akin to the elemental forces—the Fire-Being, Cthugha; the Water-Being, Cthulhu; the Lords of Air—Lloigor, Hastur the Unspeakable, Zhar, and Ithaqua; the Earth Creature, Nyarlathotep, and others—long ago cast out and imprisoned by the spells of the Elder Gods, who exist near the star Betelgueze—the Great Old Ones who have their minions, their secret followers among men and beasts, whose task it is to prepare the way for their second coming, for it is their evil intention to come again and rule the universe as once they did after their breaking away and escape from the domain of the Ancient Ones. What he told me then evoked frightening parallels to what I had read in those forbidden books at the Library of Miskatonic University only that afternoon, and he spoke in a voice of such conviction, and with such assurance, that I found myself shaken free from the orthodox learning to which I had been accustomed.

The human mind, faced with something utterly beyond its ken, inevitably reacts in one of two ways—its initial impulse is to reject in toto, its secondary to accept tentatively; but in the dread unfolding of Andrew Phelan's explanation there was the damnable, inescapable fact that only such an explanation would fit *all* the events which had taken place since his strange appearance in my room. Of the abominable tapestry of explanation which Phelan wove, several aspects were most striking, and at the same time most incredible. Dr. Shrewsbury and he, Phelan said, had been in search of the 'openings' by means of which great Cthulhu might rise from where he lies sleeping 'in his house at R'lyeh,' an undersea place, Cthulhu apparently being amphibious; under the protection of an ancient, enchanted five-pointed carven grey stone from ancient Mnar, they need not fear the minions who served the Great Old Ones —the Deep Ones, the Shoggoths, the Tcho-Tcho People, the Dholes and the Voormis, the Valusians and all similar creatures—but their activities had finally aroused the superior beings directly serving great Cthulhu, against whom the five-pointed star is powerless; therefore, Dr. Shrewsbury and he had taken flight by summoning from interstellar spaces strange bat-like creatures, the servants of Hastur, Him Who Is Not To Be Named, ancient rival of Cthulhu, and, after having partaken of a golden mead which rendered them insensible to the effects of time and space and enabled them to travel in these dimensions, while at the same time heightening their sensory perceptions to an unheard-of extent, they set out for Celaeno, where they had resumed their studies in the library of monolithic stones with books and hieroglyphs stolen from the Elder Gods by the Great Old Ones at, and subsequent to, the time of the revolt from the benign authority of those Gods. Nevertheless, though on Celaeno, they were not unaware of what took place on earth, and they had learned that commerce was again being carried on between the Deep Ones and the strange people of haunted Innsmouth—and one of those people at least was a leader in preparing the way for the return of Cthulhu. To forestall that one, Dr. Shrewsbury had sent him, Andrew Phelan, back to earth.

'What was the commerce between the Innsmouth people and the creatures who came up out of the sea to Devil Reef?'

'Surely that should have been obvious to you in Innsmouth?'

'That storekeeper said it was too much intermarriage.'

Phelan smiled grimly. 'Yes—but not among those old families of Innsmouth; it was with those evil beings from the deep, from Y'ha-nthlei below Devil Reef. And the *Esoteric Order of Dagon* is but a deceptive name for their organisation of worshippers to do the bidding of Cthulhu and his servants to prepare the way, to open the gate into this upper world for their hellish dominion!'

I pondered this shocking revelation for a full minute before I offered anything more. Accepting everything Phelan had said—and his attitude seemed to say that it made no difference to him whether or not I believed him—it would appear that, as soon as his mission had been accomplished, Phelan himself planned to return to Celaeno. I put that to him. Yes, he admitted, it was so.

'Then you already know who it is in Innsmouth who is leading the people back once more to the worship of Cthulhu and the traffic with the Deep Ones?'

'Let us say rather that I suspect; it is the evident one.'

'Ahab Marsh.'

'Ahab Marsh, yes. It was his great-grandfather, Obed, who began it, Obed with his wide travels and the strange places he visited. Obed, we know now, encountered the Deep Ones on an island in the mid-Pacific—an island where no island should have been—and he opened the way for them to come to Innsmouth. The Marshes grew wealthy, but they were no more immune to that accursed physiological change than the others in that shunned and unholy settlement. The taint is in the blood now; it has been there for generations. The events of 1928–1929 when the Federal Government invaded Innsmouth put a stop to it for only a few years, less than a decade. With the coming of Ahab Marsh—and none knows whence he came, though the two old Marsh women who were left accepted him as their own—the thing began once more, and this time less overtly, so that this time there will be no calling out to the Federals. I have come out of the sky to watch and prevent horror from being spawned again on this earth. I cannot fail; I must succeed.'

'But how?'

'Events will show. Tomorrow I am going to Innsmouth where I will continue to watch until I can take action.'

'The storekeeper told me that all outsiders are watched and regarded with suspicion.'

'But I will go in their guise.'

All that night I lay sleepless beside Andrew Phelan, torn by the desire to accompany him. If his story were the figment of his imagination, surely it was a glorious and wondrous tale, calculated to stir the pulse and fire the mind; if it were not, then with equal certainty, it was as much my responsibility as it was his to lay hands upon and destroy the evil at Innsmouth, for evil is the ancient enemy of all good, whether as we who are Christians understand it or whether as it is understood in some prehistoric mythos. My studies in divinity seemed suddenly almost frivolous in contrast to what Phelan had narrated, though I confess that at that time I still entertained doubts of some magnitude, for how could I do else? Were not the monstrous entities of evil Phelan conjured up well-nigh impossible to conceive, to say nothing of expecting belief in them? Indeed they were. Yet it is man's spiritual burden that he finds it so easy to doubt, always to doubt, and so difficult to believe even in the simplest things. And the striking parallel which forced itself upon me, a divinity student, a parallel which could not be overlooked, was plain—the similarity between the tale of the revolt of the Great Old Ones against the Elder Gods, and that other, more universally known tale of the revolt of Satan against the forces of the Lord.

In the morning I told Phelan of my decision.

He shook his head. 'It is good of you to want to help, Abel. But you have no real understanding of what it means. I've given you only a spare outline—nothing more. I would not be justified in involving you.'

'The responsibility is mine.'

'No, the responsibility is always that of the man who knows the facts. There is far more even than Dr. Shrewsbury and I already know to be learned. Indeed, I may say that we ourselves have hardly penetrated the perimeter of the whole—think, then, of how little you know!'

'I conceive it as a duty.'

He gazed at me musingly, and I saw for the first time that his eyes were far older than his thirty years. 'Let me see, you're twenty-seven now, Abel. Do you realise that if you persist in this decision, you may not have a future?'

I set out patiently to argue with him; I had already dedicated my life to the pursuit and destruction of evil, and this evil he offered me in his company was something more tangible than the evil that lurks in men's souls—he smiled and shook his head at this—and so we spent words back and forth. In the end he consented, though with a kind of cynicism I found galling.

The first step in our pursuit of the evil at Innsmouth was to shift our lodgings from Boston to Arkham, not only because of the proximity of Arkham to Innsmouth, but also because of the elimination of the risk of Phelan's being seen and recognised by my landlady, who would certainly focus highly undesirable publicity on him. And such publicity, in turn, would result in knowledge of his presence terrestrially once again being communicated to those creatures who had previously set out after Dr. Shrewsbury and Andrew Phelan and so forced their flight. No doubt the chase would begin again, in any case, but hopefully not before Phelan had accomplished what he had come back to do.

We moved that night.

Phelan did not think it wise of me to relinquish my Boston room, however; so I took a lease on it for a month—never dreaming how soon I would return to those familiar walls.

In Arkham we found a room in a comparatively new house on Curwen Street. Phelan later confided that the house stood on the site of Dr. Shrewsbury's home, which had been destroyed by fire coincident with his final disappearance. Having settled ourselves and carefully explained to our new landlady that we might be absent from our room for many hours at a time, we proceeded to assemble those properties which would be necessary for us to take up a temporary residence among the Innsmouth people—for Phelan deemed it not only wise but mandatory that, in order to remain in Innsmouth comparatively free of observation, we must be made up to look as much like the Innsmouthers as possible.

In the late afternoon of that day, Phelan set to work. I discovered in a very short time that he was a consummate artist with his hands; my features began to change utterly—from a rather innocuous-looking, and perhaps even weak-appearing young fellow, I aged skilfully and began to assume the typical narrow head, flat nose, and curious ears so common to the Innsmouth people. He worked over my entire face; my mouth thickened, my skin became coarse-pored, my colour vanished behind a grey pallor, horrible to contemplate; and he managed even to convey a bulging and batrachian expression about my eyes and to give my neck that oddly repellant appearance of having deep, almost scaly creases! I would not have known myself, after he had finished, but the operation took better than three hours, and at the end of that time it was as permanent as it could be expected to be.

'It is right,' he decided after he had examined me, and then, tirelessly, without a word, he set about to give himself a similar appearance.

Early the next morning we left the house for Innsmouth, entraining for Newburyport, and thus coming into Innsmouth on the bus from the other side, a deliberate manœuvre on Phelan's part. By noon of that day we were established, amid a few interested and curiously searching glances from the slovenly workers in the place, in the Gilman House, Innsmouth's lone open hotel—or rather, in what was left of it, for, like so many buildings in the town, it was in a very bad state of decay. We registered as Amos and John Wilken, cousins, for Phelan had discovered that Wilken was an old Innsmouth name not at present represented by any member of the family living in that accursed seaport city. The elderly clerk in the Gilman House had given us a few sharp-eyed glances, and his bulging eyes stared at the names on his register. 'Related to old Jed Wilken, be ye?' he asked. My companion nodded briskly. 'Man can see ye belong here,' the clerk said, with an almost obscene chuckle. 'Got business?'

'We're taking a little vacation,' answered Phelan.

'Come to the right place, then, ye did. Things to see here, all right, *if ye're the right kind*.'

Again that distastefully suggestive chuckle.

Once alone in our room, Phelan became more tense than ever. 'We've done well so far, but this is only the beginning. We have a good deal of work to do. I have no doubt the clerk will pass the word around that we are relatives of Jed Wilken; that will satisfy the first questions of the curious. Moreover, our appearance as "tainted", like the rest of the Innsmouthers, in the vicinity of those places where we might expect to encounter Ahab Marsh will not excite undue comment—but I am convinced that we must avoid being seen too closely by Ahab himself.'

'But what good will it do us to watch Ahab?' I countered. 'If you are already reasonably certain that it is he . . .'

'There is more to be learned about Ahab than you think, Abel. Perhaps more than I think. We know the Marsh family, we know the line, Dr. Shrewsbury and I. But nowhere in that family tree can we find any trace of a Marsh named Ahab.'

'Yet he is here.'

'Yes, indeed. But how did he come here?'

We went out soon after, having taken care to keep to old clothes, similar to those we had worn on our arrival, so that we might not give off an impression of undue affluence and so attract unwelcome attention. Phelan set out immediately for the vicinity of the waterfront, detouring only once to examine the Order of Dagon Hall at New Church Green, and ending up at last not far from the Marsh Refining Company. It was there, not long after our arrival, that I first had sight of our quarry.

Ahab Marsh was tall, though he walked in an odd, stooped manner; and his gait, too, was very strange, being not at all regular and rhythmic, but rather jerky, and even for the short distance from the refinery to the closely curtained car in which he rode, the fashion in which he made progress was very evident; his was a gait that might have been called *inhuman*, for it was not so much a walk as a kind of shuffling or lurching forward, and it was movement which had little counterpart even among the other Innsmouthers, for, whatever the changes in their aspects, their walk, shuffling as it was, was essentially human locomotion. As I have said, Ahab Marsh was taller than most of his fellow citizens, but his face was not much different from the features so common in Innsmouth, save in that it seemed somehow less coarse, and more greasy, as if the skin (for, despite its sometimes icthyic appearance, it *was* skin) were of a finer texture, this in turn suggesting that the Marsh breed was slightly superior to that of the average Innsmouther. It was impossible to see his eyes, for they were concealed by spectacles of a deep cobalt hue, and his mouth, while in many ways similar to that of the natives, was yet different in that it seemed to protrude more, doubtless because Ahab Marsh's chin receded almost into nothingness. He was, literally, a man without a chin, at sight of which I experienced a shudder of horror unlike any I had before undergone, for it gave him an appearance so frighteningly icthyic that I could not but be repelled by it. He seemed also to be earless, and wore his hat low on what appeared to be a head devoid of hair; his neck was scrawny and, though he was otherwise almost impeccably dressed, his hands were encased in black gloves, or rather, *mittens*, as I saw at second glance.

We were not observed. I had gazed at our quarry only in the most apparently casual manner, while Phelan did not look directly at him at all, but utilised a small pocket mirror to examine him even more indirectly. In a few moments Ahab Marsh had vanished into his car and driven away.

'A hot day for gloves,' was all that Phelan said.

'I thought so.'

'I fear it is as I suspected,' Phelan added then, but this he would not explain. 'We shall see.'

We repaired to another section of the city to wander through Innsmouth's narrow, shaded streets and lanes, away from the region of the Manuxet River and the falls, close to which the Marsh Refinery rose on a little bluff. Phelan walked in deep and troubled contemplation; it was evident that he was in puzzled thought, which I did not interrupt. I marvelled at the incredible state of arrested decay so prevalent in this old seaport town, and even more at the curious lack of activity; it was as if by far the majority of the inhabitants rested during the day, for very few of them were to be seen on the streets.

The night in Innsmouth, however, was destined to be different.

As darkness came, we made our way to the Order of Dagon Hall. At his one previous visit, Phelan had discovered that entrance to the hall for the ceremonies could be had only by display of a curious fish-like seal, and during the time I had tried to trace his movements here, he had fashioned several of them, of which the most perfect he had reserved for his own use, and that most closely resembling it he held for me, if I cared to use it, though he preferred that I take no such risk and remain outside the Hall.

This, however, I was unwilling to do. It was patent that a great many people were coming to the Hall, all evidently members of the *Esoteric Order of Dagon*, and I had the conviction that events I might not wish to miss might take place—this despite Phelan's insistent warning that we were placing ourselves in extreme danger by attending one of the forbidden ceremonies. Nothing daunted, I went doggedly along.

Fortunately, our seals were not challenged; I shudder to imagine what might have happened if they had been. I believe that more than anything else, our having the Innsmouth look, so skilfully fabricated, accounted for our easy passage into the Hall. We were the focus of obvious attention, but it was plain that word of our identity as members of the Wilken clan had got around, for there was neither maleficence nor challenge in the eyes of men and women who looked on occasion in our direction. We took seats near the door, meaning to be off immediately if it seemed wise to leave and, having settled ourselves, looked around the room. The hall was large and murky; its windows were shut off by black screens, apparently of tar-paper, so that it had the appearance of an old-fashioned theatre—that is, a hall converted to the showing of moving pictures when that great industry was in its infancy. Moreover, there was a brooding dusk in the room that seemed to rise from the vicinity of a small dais up front. But it was not the murkiness of the hall that seized hold of my imagination—it was the ornaments.

For the hall was decorated with strange stone carvings of fish-like beings. I recognised several of them as very similar to certain primitive sculptures which had come out of Ponape, and certain others bore a disturbing resemblance to inexplicable carvings found on Easter Island, as well as in the Mayan ruins of Central America, and the Inca remains of Peru. Even in this murky light it was clearly to be seen that these sculptures and carvings were not done by Innsmouth hands, but that they were evidently from some foreign port; indeed, they might well have come from Ponape, since the Marsh boats crossed the seas as far as the most distant corners of cilivisation. Only a very dim artificial light burned, at the foot of the stage; nothing else helped to illumine the hall, yet it seemed to me that the sculptures and bas-reliefs had a hellish suggestiveness that was soul-stirring and frightening, an out-of-this-world look which was profoundly agitating—for it spoke of time long gone by, of great ages before our time, ages when the world and perhaps the universe were young. Apart from these, and from a miniature of what must have been a vast, amorphous octopus-like creature, which occupied the centre of the dais, the hall was bare of everything in the way of decorations—nothing but rickety chairs, a plain table on the dais, and those tightly curtained windows to offset the effect of those alien bas-reliefs and sculptures, and this lack of everything only served to heighten their hideousness.

I glanced at my companion but found him gazing expressionlessly straight before him. If he had examined the bas-reliefs and sculptures, he had done so less openly. I felt that it would not be wise any longer to stare at those oddly disturbing ornaments; so I followed Phelan's example. It was still possible, however, to notice that the hall was rapidly filling up with more people than the events of the day would have persuaded me to believe still lived in the city. There were close to four hundred seats, and soon all were filled. When it became evident that there were still others to be seated, Phelan left his seat and stood up against the wall near the entrance. I did likewise, so that a pair of decrepit oldsters, hideously changed in appearance from the younger element—for the creases at their necks had grown more scaley, and were deeper, and their eyes bulged glassily—could sit down. Our relinquishment of our seats passed unnoticed, for a few others were already standing along the walls.

It must have been close to half-past nine—for the summer evening was long, and darkness did not fall early—before anything took place. Then suddenly there appeared through a rear entrance a middle-aged man clad in strangely decorated vestments; at first glance his appearance was priestly, but it was soon manifest that his vestments were blasphemously decorated, with the same batrachian and fish-like representations which in plaque and sculpture ornamented the hall. He came to the image on the dais, touched it reverently with his hands, and began to speak—not Latin or Greek, as I had at first supposed he might speak, but an odd, garbled language of which I could not understand a word, a horribly suggestive series of mouthings which immediately started a kind of low, almost lyrical humming response from the audience.

At this point Phelan touched my arm, and slipped away out of the entrance. I was meant to follow, and did so, despite my reluctance to leave the ceremonies just as they were beginning.

'What's the matter?' I asked.

'Ahab Marsh is not there.'

'He may still come.'

Phelan shook his head. 'I think not. We must look for him elsewhere.'

He walked with such purpose that I assumed, correctly, as it turned out, that he knew or suspected where he might find Ahab Marsh. I had thought that Phelan would go directly to the old Marsh home on Washington Street, but he did not; my second guess was that he would lead the way back to the Refinery, and in this I was certain that I was correct, until we reached the Refinery, crossed the bridge over the Manuxet near-by, and went on to strike out along the seashore beyond the harbour at the mouth of the river. The night was dark, save for a waning late-rising moon, pushing up out of the eastern horizon, and making its glade yellowly on the water, if feebly; stars shone above, a bank of dark clouds lay low along the southern rim of heaven, a light east wind blew.

'Do you know where you're going, Phelan?' I asked finally.

'Yes.'

We were following a little-used road which had been marked 'Private', and which led crazily along the coast there, over stones and sand, rocks and ruts. In one place Phelan dropped to his knees and lightly touched the sandy ruts.

'This road has been recently used.'

The sand was freshly disturbed, unlike the caked sand all around. 'By Ahab?' I asked.

He nodded thoughtfully. 'There is a little cove just ahead.

This is Marsh land—old Obed bought it more than a century ago.'

We hastened on, though we instinctively walked with more caution.

On the shore of the sheltered cove we found the curtained car in which Ahab Marsh had that day left the Refinery. Unafraid, perhaps because of what he knew he would find there, my companion went directly up to it. There was no one in the car, but on the back seat, thrown carelessly down, were clothes—a man's clothes—and even in the dark I recognised the suit Ahab Marsh had worn that day.

But Phelan closed the car door and hurried around to the other side, past the car down to the sea's edge, where he dropped to his knees once more and looked down. The shoes were there, I saw when I knelt at my companion's side. The socks, too—thick, woollen socks, though the day had been very warm. And the shape of the shoes in that wan moonlight was strangely upsetting—how wide they were! how curiously shaped!—at one time surely, normal shoes, if a little large, but now plainly *worn* out of shape, as if the foot inside had been—well, as if a kind of distorting disease had afflicted the wearer's feet.

And there was something else, something all the more hideously frightening in that yellow moonlight, with the sea's sound and that other sound—the sound to which Phelan cautioned me to listen: a kind of distant ululation, non-human in origin, coming not from the land at all, but from the sea, far far out, the sea—and Devil Reef, haunted in the channels of my memory by everything I had heard from that storekeeper and later on from my companion, the stories of strange, evil, unholy traffic between sea-creatures and the people of Innsmouth, the things Obed Marsh had found on Ponape and that other island, the terror of the late nineteen-twenties with the strange disappearances of young people, human sacrifices put to sea and never returned! It rose in the east and came in on the wind, a ghastly chanting that sounded like something from another world, a liquid ululation, a watery sound defying description, but evil beyond any experience of man. And it rode the wind into my horrified consciousness while my eyes were fixed still to that terrible evidence so plain on the sandy beach between the place where Ahab Marsh's shoes and socks were, and where the water began—*the footprints, not of human feet, but of pedal extremities that were squat, with elongated digits, thick, wide, and webbed!*

* * *

Of the events that came after, I hesitate to write, and yet from the moment Andrew Phelan knew, there was no need for further delay. It was Ahab Marsh who was the object of his search—and only to a considerably lesser degree the worshippers in the Order of Dagon Hall. The sacrifices, he said, had been going on again, with greater secrecy, just as in Obed Marsh's day. Ever since the debacle of 1928–1929, the Innsmouthers had been more careful, those who had been left, and those who had filtered back into the town after the Federals had gone. And Ahab—Ahab who had shed his clothing and gone into the sea only to turn up the next day, as if nothing untoward had taken place—could anyone doubt but that he had swum out to Devil Reef? And could anyone doubt what had happened to the young Innsmouth man who had driven his car that night? For that was the way of sacrifice—the chosen of Ahab, to work for Ahab and be prepared, unknowing, for the sacrifice to those hellish creatures which rose from the depths of Y'ha-nthlei beyond the shunned and feared Devil Reef which in low tide stood black and evilly above the dark waters of the Atlantic.

For Ahab Marsh was back next day, back at the Refinery, with another young man to drive his car around, and take him for those short distances from the immense old Marsh home on tree-shrouded Washington Street to the Refinery building near the falls of the Manuxet. But all night long from our room in the Gilman House we listened. It was not only the sounds from the sea, borne by the east wind, that we heard—there were other things beside that ghastly ululation. There were the terrible screams, the hoarse, animal-like screams of a man in mortal terror; there was that frightful chant which came simultaneously from the assembled members of the *Esoteric Order of Dagon*, gathered together in that Hall with its horrible sculptures and bas-reliefs and that grotesque and bestial miniature of a creature evil beyond the concept of man, that horrible mouthing which made its impact weirdly on the night air—*Ph'nglui mglw'nafh Cthulhu R'lyeh wgah'nagl fhtagn*—ever repeated, a ritual phrase which Phelan translated in his hushed voice as, 'In his house at R'lyeh dead Cthulhu waits dreaming!'

In the morning my companion went out only long enough to assure himself that Ahab Marsh had returned; then he came back to the hotel and lost himself in study, leaving me to my own devices for the remainder of that day, and adjuring me only to refrain from making myself in any way conspicuous. I had already resolved to do nothing to attract attention, but nevertheless I was determined to follow up the hints of terrible human sacrifices and horrible rites performed by certain of the Innsmouth people, which Andrew Phelan had given me; and, accordingly, I made my way back to the First National store, and Mr. Hendreson.

The storekeeper did not recognise me, which was a tribute to Phelan's skill. He adopted toward me that same servile attitude which he had used to the Waite woman who had entered his store when I was last in it, and when we were alone —for someone else was in the store at my entrance—and I attempted to identify myself, it was almost impossible to do so. Plainly, Hendreson thought at first that one of the Innsmouth people had somehow learned of our previous conversation, and it was only when I repeated to him many of the things he had said that he acknowledged me for whom I was. But he was fearful still.

'If *they* find out!' he exclaimed in a harsh, ominous whisper.

I assured him no one knew of my real identity and none would, save of course Hendreson, whom I felt certain could be trusted. He guessed that I had been 'looking into things', as he put it, and with considerable agitation again urged me to take myself off.

'Some of them seem to be able to *smell* people who don't like them. I don't know how they do it—as if they read a man's mind or his heart. And if they catch you like this—why, why . . .'

'Why what, Mr. Hendreson?'

'You'll never get back where you came from.'

I assured him with a self-confidence I was far from feeling that I had no intention of getting caught. I had come to him now for more information; despite the violent shaking of his head, I would not take his negative answer; perhaps he knew nothing, yet I must ask. Had there been any disappearances—particularly of young men and women—from Innsmouth in the years he had been here?

He nodded furtively.

'Many?'

'Maybe twenty or so. When the Order meets—they don't meet often; it usually comes out after that. On the nights the Order meets, somebody just isn't heard from again. *They* say they've run away. First few times I heard it, I didn't find that hard to believe; I could understand why they'd want to run away from Innsmouth.' But then—there were those other things—the people who disappeared usually always worked for Ahab Marsh, and there were those old stories about Obed Marsh—how he carried people out to Devil Reef and came back alone. Zadok Allen had talked about it; *they* said Zadok was crazy, but Zadok said things, and there was certain clinching evidence to support what the crazed old man said. He talked like that, and he had spells, Hendreson said, until he—*died*. By the way he said it, I gathered that Zadok Allen had not just died.

'You mean until they killed him,' I countered.

'I didn't say so; I'm not the one to say anything. Mind you, I never *saw* a thing—anyway, nothing you could make something of. I never saw anyone disappear; I just didn't see them any more, that's all. Later on, I heard about it—somebody dropped a word about it here and there, and I picked it up. Nothing ever got into the paper; nothing ever was said so it could; no one ever made any search or any attempt to get trace of the missing ones. I couldn't help thinking about the stories old Zadok Allen and those others whispered about Captain Obed Marsh. Might be it's all in my mind. It would affect a man's mind to live in a place like this for as many years as I've been here; it would affect some men in just as many months. I'm not the one to say old Zadok Allen was crazy. All I say is that I don't think he was, and he never talked much until he had a little something to drink; that loosened his tongue, and usually next time he was sober he seemed to be mighty sorry he said anything, walking along and looking over his shoulder all the time even in broad daylight, and always a-looking out toward the sea, out to where you can just see the line of Devil Reef when the tide is low and the day is clear. The Innsmouthers don't look out there much, but sometimes when there's a meeting at the Order of Dagon Hall, there are lights out there, strange lights, and there are lights from the cupola of the old Gilman House, just flashing back and forth—as if it was talk going on between 'em.'

'You've seen those lights yourself?'

'It's the only thing I've seen. Might be a boat, but I don't think so. Not out there at Devil Reef.'

'Have you ever been out there?'

He shook his head. 'No, sir. Don't have any wish to go. I got close to it one time in a launch—ugly grey stone, with some mighty strange shapes to it—and I didn't want to get any closer. It was just like something driving you away, like a big hand reaching out invisible and pushing you back—that's the way it was. Made my skin crawl and my hair tingle along the back of my neck. I never forgot it—and that was before I heard much; so I never put it down to what was suggested or hinted at and something getting to work on my nerves or my imagination.'

'Ahab Marsh is the power here in Innsmouth then?'

'That he is. That's because there's not a Waite or a Gilman or an Orne left, not a man, that is, just the women, and they're growing old. The men all vanished about the time the Federals came in here.'

I turned him back to the subject of those mysterious disappearances. It seemed incredible that young men and women could simply drop out of existence in this day and age, and never a word of it printed anywhere. Oh, responded Hendreson, I didn't know Innsmouth if I thought that was impossible. They were close-mouthed, close as clams, and if they figured it was something they had to do for their pagan god or whatever it was they worshipped, they never complained, they just took it and made the best of it, and they were all mortally afraid of Ahab Marsh. He came close to me, so close that I was aware of his quickened pulse.

'I touched him once, just once, and that once was enough! God! He was cold, cold as ice, and where I touched him, between the end of his glove and his coat-sleeve—he drew back right away and gave me a look—the skin was moist-cold, like a fish!' He shuddered at the memory of it, touched a handkerchief to his temples, and broke away.

'Aren't they all like that?'

'No, they're not. The others are different. They say the Marshes were all cold-blooded, especially since Captain Obed's time, but I've heard different. You take that fellow—Williamson, I think his name was—who brought the Federals here. They didn't know it at that time, but he was a Marsh—he had Orne blood in him, too, and when *they* found it out, they just waited for him to come back. And he did come. He came back, they said, and he went right down to the water, a-singing, they said, and he took off his clothes and he dove in and began swimming out toward that reef, and never a word of him since. Mind you, I didn't see it myself; it's just what I heard, though it took place in my own time. Those with Marsh blood in 'em always come back, no matter how far away they are. Look at Ahab Marsh—come from God knows where.'

Once started, Hendreson proved to be unusually loquacious, despite his fears. Doubtless the long periods of abstinence in his conversation with outsiders had something to do with it, as well as the security his shop afforded him, for it was not often visited in the morning hours; the Innsmouth people preferred to shop in late afternoon, and he was often obliged to keep his store open beyond the usual six o'clock closing hour. He talked of the strange jewellery worn by the Innsmouthers—those grotesque and repulsive amulets and tiaras, the rings and pectorals, with repellent figures cut in high relief on them all. I could not doubt that they were the same as those figures of the bas-reliefs and sculptures in the Order of Dagon Hall; Hendreson has seen pieces on occasion; those who belonged to the Order wore them, and certain of the debased churches had them, too. He spoke about the sounds from the sea—'a kind of singing, and it's no human voice does it.'

'What is it?'

'I don't know. No inclination to find out, either. It wouldn't be healthy. It comes from somewhere out there—like last night.' His voice dropped to a whisper.

'I know what you mean.'

He hinted at the other sounds; though he did not once mention the hoarse, terrified screams, he had nonetheless heard them. And there were other things, he muttered darkly, things far more terrible, things that went back to old Obed Marsh and still lived in the waters beyond Devil Reef. There was that suppressed talk about Obed himself—how he was not really dead, how a party of boating people from Newburyport way who knew the Marsh family came into port one day all pale and shaking and said they had seen Obed out there, swimming like a porpoise, and if it was not Obed Marsh, then what was it in his likeness? What was it the Newburyporters had seen? No plain fish would scare men and women like that! And why did the Innsmouthers try so hard to keep it quiet? They shut up the Newburyport people, all right—probably because they were strangers and they didn't really want to believe what it was they saw out there near Devil Reef. But there *were* things swimming out there, others had seen them, things that dove and disappeared and never came up again, though they looked like men and women, except that they were sometimes scaley and with odd, wrinkled, and shiny skin. And what happened to so many of the old folks? There never seemed to be funerals, nor buryings—but certain of them got queerer-looking every year, and then one fine day went down to the sea and first thing people knew they were reported 'lost at sea' or 'drowned' or something like that. It was true, the things swimming in the sea were not often seen by day—but at night! And what was it, what manner of creature was it that came climbing out of the sea on to Devil Reef? And why did certain of the Innsmouthers go out there in the night? He seemed to grow more and more excited as he talked, though his voice grew more hushed, and it was patently clear that he had brooded a great deal about everything he had heard since he came to Innsmouth, and was held to it by a fascination over which he had no control, a fascination which existed side by side with an utter and almost morbid loathing.

It was almost noon when I made my way back to the Gilman House.

My companion had finished his study, and he now listened to what I had to say with the utmost gravity, though I could detect nothing in his attitude to reveal that he had not previously been aware of what Hendreson had said and hinted. After I finished, he said nothing, only nodded, and went on to explain our coming movements. Our period of stay in Innsmouth was almost over, he said; we would leave the city just as soon as we had dealt with Ahab Marsh, and that might be tonight, it might be tomorrow night, but it would be soon, for all was in readiness. Meanwhile, however, there were certain aspects of this strange pursuit of which I must know, and chief among them was the danger to myself.

'I am not afraid,' I hastened to say.

'No, perhaps not in the physical sense. But it is impossible to say what they might do to you. All of us carry a talisman which is potent against the Deep Ones and the minions of the Old Ones, but not against the Old Ones themselves, or their immediate servitors, who also come to the surface of earth on special missions to destroy such of us as learn the secrets and oppose the coming again of great Cthulhu, and those others.'

So saying, he placed before me a small, five-pointed star made of a stone material foreign to me. A grey stone—and instantly I remembered reading of it in the Library at Miskatonic University—'the five-pointed star carven of grey stone from ancient Mnar!' which had the power of the Elder Ones in its magic. I took it wordlessly and put it into my pocket, as Phelan indicated I should.

He went on.

This might afford me partial terrestrial protection, but there was a way of further escape if danger from the immediate servitors of Cthulhu menaced. I, too, might come to Celaeno, if I wished, though the way was terrible, and it would be required of me that I enlist the aid of creatures who, while in opposition to the Deep Ones and all others who served Great Cthulhu, were themselves essentially evil, for they served Hastur the Unspeakable, laired in the black Lake of Hali in the Hyades. In order that these creatures be made to serve me, however, it would be necessary for me to swallow a small pellet, a distillation of that marvellous golden mead of Professor Shrewsbury's, the mead which rendered the drinker insensible to the effects of time and space, and enabled him to travel in those dimensions, while at the same time heightening his sensory perceptions; then to blow upon a strange stone whistle, and also to call forth into space certain words: '*Iä! Iä! Hastur, Hastur, cf'syak 'vulgtmm, vugtlagln, vulgtmm!*

Ai! Ai! Hastur!' Certain flying creatures—the Byakhee—would come out of space, and I was to mount and take flight unafraid. But only if danger pressed close—for the danger of the Deep Ones and all who are allied to them, insisted Phelan, is as great to the soul as to the body.

To all this I listened in amazement not untouched by a kind of spiritual terror—that terror so common to men who, for the first time look out into the void of greater space, who begin to contemplate seriously for the initial time the vastness of the outer universes—a terror induced by the instinctive knowledge that it was by this means of travel that Andrew Phelan had reached my room in Boston, and it was by this means that he had originally gone forth more than a year ago!

So saying, Phelan gave into my hands the little golden pellets, three of them, in case I should lose one, and also a tiny whistle, which he warned me never to blow upon save in the dire need he had outlined, unless I were prepared for fateful consequences. This much, he said, he could do for my protection, and he made it plain that we would not be returning to Arkham together, though we might set out for that town in each other's company.

'They will expect us to go back to Newburyport,' he said. 'So we will follow the railroad tracks toward Arkham. That is shorter, in any case, and by the time they may be ready to pursue, we should be well out of their way. Immediately our work is done, we will make for the railroad; we will wait long enough to be sure that our work here is accomplished.' He paused significantly and then added that pursuit from Innsmouth by the people themselves we need not fear.

'What other then?'

'When that other comes, you will know without prior explanation,' he answered ominously.

By nightfall, we were prepared. I did not as yet fully know Andrew Phelan's plan, but I knew that the first step necessary would be to empty the Washington Street house of the Marshes of the two women who were there. To this end Phelan sent them a prosaic note saying that an elderly relative had arrived to put up at the Gilman House, and, being in ill health and unable to call, would enjoy a visit that evening at nine o'clock from the Misses Aliza and Ethlai Marsh. It was a commonplace letter, correct in every detail, save that my companion embellished it with a reproduction of that seal of Dagon, and again impressed the seal in wax upon the flap of the envelope. He had signed the name of Wilken, knowing that there had years ago been marriage between the Marshes and the Wilkens, and he felt certain that this letter would take the Marsh women from the house for the length of time required for what must be done to destroy the leadership of the minions of Cthulhu at Innsmouth and so retard whatever progress had been made in preparing the way for the rising again, the coming from his house of that dread being dreaming deep in the waters under the earth.

He dispatched this letter near supper-time, and instructed the desk clerk that if anyone should telephone, he would be back directly. Then we went out, Phelan carrying a little valise into which he had put some of the things he had brought with him in the pockets of that robe he had worn on his arrival.

The sky was overcast, which my companion was pleased to see, for at nine there would otherwise still have been some twilight; now, however, at that hour, the night would be dark enough for our purpose. If all went as he hoped, the Marsh women would travel to the Gilman House by car, driven by the new man; that would leave Ahab alone in that old mansion. Phelan explained that he had no qualms; if the women did not respond to that message, they too must be destroyed, much as he disliked the thought of proceeding against them in the same fashion as against Ahab. We had no difficulty in finding a place of adequate concealment from which we could watch the Washington Street house, for the street was heavily grown with trees, thus affording shadows and dark corners. The house across the way was shrouded in darkness, save for a tiny light that gleamed in a room on the second floor, but just before nine o'clock, a light went up downstairs.

'They're coming,' whispered my companion.

He was right, for in a few moments that black, curtained car rolled around to the front entrance, and the two Marsh women, heavily veiled, came from the house and, entering the car, drove away.

Phelan lost not an instant. He crossed the street into the dark grounds of the Marsh estate, and there at once opened his valise, which contained scores of the five-pointed stars, all very small. These, he said, were to be used to circle the house, particularly in the vicinity of the doors and windows; we must work silently and swiftly, for if these talismans were not laid down, Ahab might escape. But he could not cross these stones, he could not pass by them in any way. I hastened to do Phelan's bidding, and soon met him coming around the other way. The darkness was urgent with foreboding; at any moment the Marsh women might come back; at any second Ahab Marsh might become aware of someone in the grounds, though we made no sound.

'It will soon be over,' said Phelan then. 'Whatever happens, be still—do not be alarmed.'

He then disappeared once more around to the back of the house. He was gone but a few minutes before he returned to where I stood in the shadow of a bush near the front entrance. But he did not pause; he went on up to the front door and there busied himself for a few moments. When he stepped away, I saw a thin flame growing at one corner of the door—he had fired the house!

He joined me, looking grimly and emotionlessly toward that single window where light burned. 'Only fire will destroy them,' he said. 'You might remember that, Abel. You may encounter them again.'

'We'd better get away.'

'Wait. We must make sure of Ahab.'

The fire ate rapidly at the old wood, and already at the rear of the house the flames lit up the close-pressing trees. At any moment someone might see, someone might give the alarm which would summon the rickety old Innsmouth fire department vehicles; but in this we were fortunate, for the Innsmouthers generally shunned the places where Ahab Marsh lived and worked, fearing and respecting the Marshes, even as their ancestors had feared and respected those earlier members of that accursed family who had trafficked with beings out of the sea and so had brought into this seaport town a blight of horrible miscegenation which had left its mark upon all their progeny.

Suddenly the window of that lit room was thrown open, and Ahab leaned out. He was there for but an instant; then he withdrew, not troubling to shut the window, and thus creating an effective draught for the flames from below.

'Now!' whispered Andrew Phelan urgently.

The front door was torn open, and Ahab Marsh bounded out past the flames in one great leap. But he went no farther; he came down, took one step, and then recoiled, his arms upflung, and a horrible, guttural cry welled from his thick lips. Behind him the flames mounted and spread, aided by the draught through the open door; already the heat must have been awful where he stood—for what happened then is seared upon my consciousness for all time.

The clothes worn by Ahab Marsh began to fall from him in flames as he stood there—first those curious mittens on his hands, then the black skull-cap, and the clothes about his body—and this so swiftly that he seemed literally to burst from his clothes! What stood there then was not human, it was not a man, it was a hellish batrachian and icthyic travesty of a man, whose hands were froglike and webbed, great pads instead of hands, whose body was scaled and tentacled and gleamed with the moisture so natural to its coldness—a body which had been bound into the unnatural clothing of a human being, but which, now that that clothing had fallen away, and the tight linens binding it to fit into that clothing as well, resembled a thing out of an unknown, dark corner of earth's forbidden places—a terrible, ghastly thing that walked in the guise of a man, but had gills beneath the wax ears which melted off in the heat of that destructive fire where that creature slowly backed into the flames, rather than dare the power of those stones laid end to end around the house, whimpering and crying bestially, in a kind of ululation I had heard before!

Small wonder Ahab Marsh had been able to swim from shore out to Devil Reef! Small wonder he had carried sacrifices to the waiting hosts out there in the depths! For the creature in the guise and identity of Ahab Marsh was not a Marsh at all, he was not a human being; *the thing that called itself Ahab Marsh, the thing the Innsmouth people so blindly followed was one of the Deep Ones itself, come from the sunken city of Y'ha-nthlei to resume again the work once begun by the terrible Obed Marsh at the behest and bidding of the minions of Great Cthulhu!*

As in a dream I felt Andrew Phelan's touch upon my arm; I turned and followed him into the shadowed street, down which even now came that curtained car carrying the Marsh women back to that unhallowed house. We fled, skulking in the shadows. There was no need to return to the Gilman House, for we had left money in our room to pay for our lodgings, and nothing of importance in personal belongings had been left there. We went directly toward the railroad tracks and made our way out of that justly shunned city.

A mile beyond the town we turned and looked back. The redness of the sky in that place told us what was happening; the fire in that ancient tinder house had spread to neighbouring houses. But something of even more portentous significance took place, for silently my companion pointed seaward, and there, far out on the rim of the sky, I saw strange, green flashes of light and, looking swiftly back toward Innsmouth, I saw other lights flashing from a high place which could have been none other than the cupola of the Gilman House.

Then Andrew Phelan took my hand. 'Goodbye, Abel. I am

going to leave you here. You will remember everything I have said.'

'But they will find you!' I cried.

He shook his head. 'You go on along the tracks; lose no time. I'll be all right.'

I did as I was bidden, knowing that every moment's delay was potentially fatal.

I could not have gone far when I heard that strange, unearthly whistling sound, and shortly thereafter the voice of Andrew Phelan shouting triumphantly into space—*'Iä! Iä! Hastur! Hastur cf'ayak 'vulgtmm, vugtlagln, vulgtmm! Ai! Ai! Hastur!'*

Involuntarily I turned.

There, silhouetted against the red-hued sky over Innsmouth, I saw a great flying thing, a great bat-like bird that came sweeping down and was lost briefly in the darkness—the Byakhee! Then it rose up again, and it was not alone—something more was there between its great wings where it mounted swiftly out of sight.

Daring danger, I ran back.

Of Andrew Phelan there was no sign.

* * *

It is now almost a fortnight since the events of that week.

The divinity school has known me no more; I have been haunting the Library of Miskatonic University, and I have learned more—much more—about things Andrew Phelan would not tell me, and I understand better now what it was that went on in accursed Innsmouth, things that are going on in other remote corners of this earth, which is always and forever a great battleground for the forces of good and those of evil.

Two nights ago for the first time I saw that I was being followed. Perhaps I was wrong in tearing from my face all those disfiguring things Andrew Phelan had put there to give me 'the Innsmouth look', and leaving them lie along the little-used tracks in the direction of Arkham, where they might be found. Perhaps it was not the Innsmouth people who found them—but something other, something that came out of the sea that night in response to those signals from the cupola of the Gilman House. Yet my follower of two nights ago was an Innsmouth man, surely; his oddly batrachian appearance was unmistakable. Of him, however, I had no fear; I had the five-pointed star-stone in my pocket; I felt safe.

But last night came the other!

Last night I heard the earth move under me! I heard the sound of great, sluggish, sucking footsteps slogging along in the waters of the earth, and I knew what Andrew Phelan meant when he said that I would know when that other pursuer came! I know!

I have made haste to put this down, and I will send it to the Library at Miskatonic University, to be put with Dr. Shrewsbury's papers and what they call the 'Phelan Manuscript', written by Andrew Phelan before he went to Celaeno for the first time. It is late, and I have the conviction that I am not alone; there is an unnatural hush about the entire city, and I can hear those horrible sucking sounds from far beneath. In the east, the Pleiades and Celaeno have begun to rise above the horizon. I have taken the little golden pellet made from Dr. Shrewsbury's mead, I have the whistle here beside me, I remember the words, and if the heightening of awareness that is certain to follow the taking of the mead discloses something of what it is that dogs me now, I shall know what to do.

Even now I am becoming aware of changes within me. It is as if the walls of the house fell away, as if the street too, were gone, and a fog—something in that watery fog, like a giant frog with tentacles—like a—

Great God! What horror!

Iä! Iä! Hastur! . . .

The one author above all others whose name is synonymous with tales of Satanism is *Dennis Wheatley*. His various books on Black Magic are read and admired around the world for their story-telling ability and authenticity. Yet despite this, Wheatley openly admits he has never actually witnessed Satanists at their dark rites. 'All the data that went into my novels,' he says, 'has been acquired from old treatises or from long conversations with famous occultists to whom I had secured introductions. My practical knowledge of Magic is absolutely nil and, to this day, I have never attended an occult ceremony, because I believe it to be dangerous to do so.' This same philosophy, however, has not been observed by the most famous self-confessed devil worshipper of modern times, Aleister Crowley. In his writings—and numerous lurid newspaper and magazine articles—Crowley ('The Great Beast' as he called himself) admitted to practising Satanism, conducting occult rituals and even performing sacrifices with small animals. I am therefore particularly pleased to present the following tale which has Wheatley writing about Crowley—the encounter, I think you will agree, is a fascinating one. In 'The Black Magician' you will meet an occult investigator, Colonel Verney (known as C.B.), who goes to the home of a clergyman suspected of being a secret Satanist. C.B. is endeavouring to trap the man into a confession of his activities. . . .

The Black Magician

DENNIS WHEATLEY

The rain was still falling in a steady downpour, and now that the light was failing the little turrets surmounting the steep gables roofing the house presented only a blurred outline. As C.B. squelched his way up the garden path the coppice twenty yards away on his right was already pitch-dark, but to his left the tall, ancient yews of the churchyard still stood out, like sombre sentinels guarding the dead, against the heavy grey sky that presaged a night of inky blackness.

Under the Gothic porch there lingered enough light for him to make out a scrolled iron bell-pull beside an arched front door of solid oak and studded with massive nail-heads making a curious pattern. He jerked it vigorously and heard the bell clang hollowly in a distant part of the house. No approaching footsteps told him that anyone was on the way to answer it, but after a moment the door swung silently open on well-oiled hinges.

Framed against the dim light from a Moorish lantern that hung in the centre of a small square hall stood a manservant of a type that one would hardly have expected to find in an Essex village. He wore a red fez and was robed in a white burnous. His skin was very dark, but only his thick lips suggested negro blood; and C.B. put him down at once as an Egyptian. Crossing his black hands on his chest he made a deep bow, then waited silently until C.B. asked:

'Is Canon Copely-Syle in?'

The man salaamed again and replied in excellent English, a

slight lisp alone betraying his foreign origin, 'My master has just settled down to his writing, and at such times he is averse to being disturbed. But if you will give me your name, sir, I will enquire if he is willing to receive you.'

'My name is Verney; but that won't convey anything to him. Just say that I have come here as a Seeker after Truth.'

As C.B. spoke he stepped into the hall and the Egyptian closed the door. His felt slippers making no sound on the tiled floor and his white robe billowing out behind him, he seemed almost to float away down the corridor. Two minutes later he returned; his white teeth flashed in a smile, he bowed and murmured, 'Allow me, sir, to take your things. Then if you will follow me . . .'

Having divested himself of his wet coat, C.B. was led to the back of the house and shown into a room that, unlike the appearance of the house itself and the Egyptian servant, had nothing even suggestive of the sinister about it. In fact it might well have been the workroom of a wealthy but unimaginative clergyman. Wealthy, because of the great array of valuable books that covered all its walls from floor to ceiling: unimaginative, because its owner was evidently content to have left unchanged its Victorian décor and hideous furnishings of elaborately carved light oak. Nevertheless, it had an air of solid comfort. It was a large room, but the fact that it was not very lofty made it cosier than it would otherwise have been. The light from three standard lamps shone warmly on the gilding of the books and a big log fire blazed on an open hearth. In front of it stood the Canon.

He was shortish and plump both in face and figure. His cheeks were rosy but tended to sag a little; the rest of his skin had such a childlike pinkness that it was difficult to visualise him ever having the need to shave. His forehead was broad and smooth; his long silver hair swept back from it to fall in curls on the nape of his neck, but gave no impression of untidiness, suggesting rather the elegance of a Georgian parson. His eyes were hazel, but very pale, and his expression benign.

His features were well cut, the only thing unpleasant about them being an exceptionally thick and out-jutting lower lip. He was dressed in a black frock-coat, ribbed satin vest, clerical collar, breeches, gaiters and black shoes with silver buckles; all of which added to the impression that he was a divine of a past generation.

Stepping forward, he smiled and extended a plump hand.

His smile detracted from the pleasantness of his expression, as it revealed a lower row of blackened, uneven teeth. His hand was slightly damp and so soft as to seem almost boneless. C.B. found its touch so repulsive that he had to restrain himself from withdrawing his own unduly quickly.

The Canon pushed a big horsehair-covered armchair a little nearer to the fire and murmured, 'Sit down, Mr. Verney. Sit down and warm yourself.' Then he bustled over to a table on which stood an array of drinks, and added, 'A whisky and soda now? You must need it after your chilly journey.'

C.B. would have preferred to accept neither food nor drink while in that house, but as his object was to win Copely-Syle's confidence he accepted, and, producing his pipe, said, 'D'you mind if I smoke?'

'No, no. Please do.' The Canon carried over two whiskies, handed one to his caller.

'Although you may not remember it, we've met before,' C.B. said after a while, the business of filling his pipe now complete.

'Have we? Where?'

'I can't remember exactly, but I know it was with Aleister Crowley.'

'That charlatan! I hardly knew him.'

With the object of passing himself off as a brother initiate in the Black Art, C.B. had risked a shot in the dark. He had felt confident that anyone of Copely-Syle's age and interests must have come into contact with the infamous Crowley at one time or another, and, although the Canon's reactions were disappointing, he could not now go back on his statement. To get a firmer ground, he began to reminisce about the dead magician.

'If you had known Aleister as well as I did, you certainly wouldn't dub him a charlatan. Of course in his later years he couldn't have harmed a rabbit; everyone knew that. The poor old boy degenerated into a rather pathetic figure, and was reduced to sponging on all and sundry in order to keep body and soul together. But when he was a young man it was a very different story. He unquestionably had power, and there were very few things of this world that he could not get with it. Even as an undergraduate he showed how far advanced he was along the Left Hand Path. You must have heard about the Master of John's refusing to let him put on a bawdy Greek play, and how he revenged himself. He made a wax image of the Master and took it out to a meadow one night with some friends when the moon was at the full. They formed the usual circle and Crowley recited the incantation. He was holding the needle and meant to jab it into the place that was the equivalent of the image's liver, but at the critical moment one of his pals got the wind up and broke the circle. Crowley's hand was deflected and the needle pierced the image's left ankle. That was a bit of luck for the Master of John's. Instead of dying of a tumour on the liver, he only slipped and broke his left ankle when coming down the college steps next day. Up to then Crowley's friends had regarded the whole business as a joke spiced with a vague sort of wickedness; but afterwards they were scared stiff of him, and naturally they were much too impressed to keep their mouths shut; so the facts are known beyond any shadow of doubt.'

Copely-Syle shrugged slightly. 'Of course, it's perfectly possible, and I do remember hearing about it now. But the story can be no more than hearsay as far as you are concerned. You are much too young to have been up at Cambridge with Crowley.'

'Oh yes. I didn't meet him till years later, when he was in middle life and at the height of his powers.' After pausing for a moment C.B. added the glib lie, 'I was initiated by him at the Abbaye de Thelema.'

'Really? I was under the impression that Crowley did no more than use his reputation as a mystic to lure young neurotics there, and kept the place going as a private brothel for his own enjoyment.'

'Most of its inmates were young people, and as the whole of his teaching was summed up in "Do what thou wilt shall be the whole of the Law" a state of general promiscuity naturally followed from it. New brothers and sisters soon lost their shyness, and after that he had little difficulty in persuading them to participate in sexual orgies when the stars were propitious for the performance of special rites. But you can take it from me that he knew his stuff, and that the perversions practised under his auspices were only a means to an end. You must know as well as I do that certain types of Satanic entity feed upon the emanations given out by humans while engaged in the baser forms of eroticism. As far as Crowley was concerned the orgies were simply the bait that lured such entities to the Abbaye and enabled him to gain power over them.'

The Canon had sat down again. He now appeared deeply interested as he said, 'You are really convinced that he conducted Satanic rituals with intent, and not merely performed some mumbo-jumbo as an excuse to possess a series of young women?'

'Each of his rituals was performed with a definite intention. Of that I am certain, and I know that many of them produced the desired result. He always insisted on everyone present behaving with the greatest solemnity, and when celebrating pagan rites he was most impressive. He could even render the receiving of the osculam infame a gesture of some dignity, and his memory was prodigious; so he experienced no difficulty at all in reciting the lines of the Roman communion backwards.'

'In Christian countries there are few ceremonies more potent than the Black Mass; but from my memory of him I am much surprised to learn from you that he ever proved capable of celebrating that mystery.'

'I have never seen it better done,' C.B. averred seriously. 'Although, of course, he was not able to fulfil the technical requirements in their entirety.'

'You mean that among the women neophytes there was never a virgin who could be used as an altar?'

'No, I didn't mean that. It's true that on most occasions he had to make do with young women who had already been seduced, but twice while I was there he managed to get hold of a virgin. And naturally there was no difficulty about holy wafers for desecration and that sort of thing. I was simply referring to the fact that to be one hundred per cent potent the celebrant should have been a Roman Catholic priest, and Crowley had never been ordained.'

'Quite, quite. That was a pity, but would be overlooked if suitable propitiation were made to the Prince by way of blood offerings. Did Crowley—er—ever achieve the apotheosis in that direction?'

'I can't say for certain. In medieval times life was held so cheap that adepts such as Gilles de Rais could decimate a dozen parishes for the furtherance of their magical operations, and no one powerful enough to interfere felt sufficiently strongly about it to do so. But in these days matters are very different. The Italian police must have had a pretty shrewd idea of the sort of thing that went on at the Abbaye; but they were a tolerant lot and were well bribed to keep their ideas to themselves, so they never gave us any trouble. I'm sure they would have, though, had they had the least grounds to suppose that we were offering up human sacrifices. Usually Crowley used cats or goats, and once I was present when a monkey was crucified upside down. After I had left I heard rumours that one or two children had disappeared from villages round about; but I'm inclined to suppose that was simply malicious gossip put about by Crowley's enemies.'

The pale eyes of Copely-Syle had a faraway look as he murmured thoughtfully, 'Ah, for the culminating act in such rituals there is nothing so efficacious as the warm blood of an unweaned child.'

C.B. had to bite hard on the stem of his pipe to repress a shudder; but he felt that he was now well on the way to achieving his object in going there, which was to establish such an apparent community of interests with the Canon that the latter would voluntarily give himself away. For a few moments they both sat staring silently into the fire, then the Canon said:

'From all you say, Crowley must have reached at least the degree of Magus, if not Ipsissimus. What I cannot understand is how by the middle nineteen-thirties, when I met him, he should have degenerated into an impotent windbag, incapable of impressing anyone except a handful of credulous old women.'

'That is easily explained. It was that unfortunate affair in Paris towards the end of the nineteen-twenties. You are right in supposing that before that he ranked as an Ipsissimus, but that night he was cast right back across the Abyss. In fact, he was stripped of all his powers and afterwards the most callow neophyte could have bested him in an astral conflict.'

'What an awful thing to happen to an adept,' said the Canon a shade uneasily. 'Did he then recant and offer to make a full confession in exchange for being accepted back into the Church? I can imagine no other act deserving of such terrible punishment.'

'Oh no, it was nothing like that. It was simply that his ambition was so great that he overreached himself. If he could have bent Pan to his will he would have been the most powerful being on earth. With Pan's pipes playing as he directed he could have made even governments dance to his tune. He attempted to master Pan, but he wasn't quite strong enough; so he paid the price of failure: that's all.'

'I find this most interesting,' said Copely-Syle in a low voice. 'Do you happen to know any details of what took place?'

'Yes. As a matter of fact I was still one of his disciples and with him at the time.' C.B. was on safer ground now, as he had actually had a first-hand account of this grim affair from one of Crowley's young men, and he went on:

'The attempt took place in Paris. Crowley made up a coven, so including himself there were thirteen of us; and in this instance we were naturally all males. We were staying at an hotel on the Left Bank. The proprietor was an initiate, and it was quite a small place; so we took the whole premises for the night, and all the servants were got rid of from midday to midday. There was a big room at the top of the house which seemed just the thing for the purpose. In the afternoon we moved out every scrap of furniture and cleaned it with the utmost thoroughness. Then in the evening all of us assisted at the purificatory rites; but fortunately, as it turned out, Crowley had decided that only his senior disciple, a chap who had taken the name of McAleister, should assist him at the actual evocation.

'At ten o'clock the rest of us robed them, then left them there, and Crowley locked the door behind us. He had already issued strict injunctions that whatever sounds we might hear coming from the room, even if they were cries for help, we were in no circumstances to attempt to enter it; as such cries might be a trick of Pan's made in an endeavour to evade him, and any interruption of the ritual would render the spell abortive. We had fasted all day, so our associate, the landlord, had prepared an excellent cold buffet for us downstairs in the dining-room. It wasn't a very gay meal, as all of us were aware of the magnitude of the task the Master Therion had set himself. We had great confidence in his powers, but it was probably several centuries since any adept had had the audacity to attempt to summon the Horned God in person, so we were naturally a bit nervy.

'It was just on midnight when we heard the first noises upstairs. There were thumpings and shouts, then all Hell seemed to break loose. Piercing screams were mingled with what sounded like sacks of potatoes being flung about. We had the impression that the whole building was rocking. In fact it was, as the chandelier above us began to swing, the glasses jingled on the sideboard and a picture fell from the wall with a loud crash. It was like being in the middle of an earthquake, and the room in which we were sitting had suddenly become icy cold.

'We had all been inmates of the Abbaye at one time or another and had passed pretty severe tests in standing up to Satanic manifestations, so we were by no means a chicken-hearted lot. But on this occasion we were seized by abject terror, and none of us made the least effort to hide it. We just sat there, white to the gills and paralysed by the thought that at any second the terrible Being up above might descend on us.

'After a few moments the pandemonium subsided, and we tried to pull ourselves together. With our teeth chattering from the cold, we debated whether we had not better ignore Crowley's orders and go up to find out what had happened. But the room began to get warm again and that, together with the continued silence, led us to hope that Crowley had won his battle and succeeded in binding Pan. If so, for us to have gone in then might still have ruined everything, and Crowley's rage would have been beyond all reckoning. Knowing his powers, none of us felt inclined to risk the sort of punishment he might have inflicted on us for disobeying him; so we decided to let matters be, and I for one was not sorry about that.

'We were all too scared to face the solitude of going to bed, and started to drink in an attempt to keep our spirits up; but that didn't work. Somehow we couldn't even get tight, and we sat on hour after hour, hardly speaking.

'At last that miserable night ended. Dawn came and we began to hope that Crowley would soon come down, his fat face beaming with triumph, to make our fears seem ridiculous; but he didn't. We waited till seven o'clock. There was still not a sound from the top of the house, so by then we felt that we were no longer justified in evading the issue. All the same, we didn't exactly run upstairs, as by that time we were feeling pretty apprehensive about what we might find when we got there. For a moment or two all eleven of us stood huddled on the top of the landing, listening; but with the early morning noises coming up from the street we could not definitely make out any sound coming from the room. Someone suggested that after their exhausting ordeal Crowley and McAleister might still be sleeping, and the idea gave us fresh hope for the moment; but another fellow knocked hard on the door, and there was no reply. That left us with no alternative but to break down the door.'

Like the good raconteur that he was, C.B. paused to knock out his pipe. Copely-Syle jerked his head forward and exclaimed in a breathless whisper, 'Go on, man! Go on! What did you find?'

C.B. looked him straight in the eyes, and, certain of his facts on this final point, said quietly, 'McAleister was dead. He was stretched out on his back with his arms flung wide, absolutely rigid, just as though he had been electrocuted, and with an appalling look of stark horror on his face such as I never wish to see again. Crowley's pontifical robes were scattered in ribbons about the floor. It looked as if they had been ripped from his body by some ferocious animal. He was crouching in a corner naked. He didn't know any of us. He had become a gibbering idiot.'

The Canon took a quick gulp at his drink and muttered, 'Horrible, horrible! Have you any idea what went wrong?'

'No, none of us had. We could only suppose that McAleister had been unable to take it, and cracked at the critical moment. Crowley was in a private asylum outside Paris for six months. He was very lucky to recover his sanity, and afterwards he would never speak of the affair. In fact, I doubt very much if he had any definite memory of what had happened. But you'll understand now why from that time on he seemed like a washed-out rag, and why when you met him he entirely failed to impress you.'

'Yes, yes indeed,' the Canon said, his eyes now wild and on fire. 'I was not introduced to him until the early 'thirties, and what you have told me explains the disappointment I felt at the time.

'But I have misjudged him. He was indeed a true Brother in Evil with us all!'

And even as he knew, finally, that all his suspicions about the Canon were true, C.B. was unable to restrain the terrible shudder which shook his frame.

The notorious *Aleister Crowley*, about whom you have just read, was himself a writer and completed a number of novels and treatises based on his lifelong search for the true meanings of Satanism and the Occult. Although I have read much of Crowley's fiction I can find no extract which suits the particular requirements of this book. However, there recently came into my possession a copy of one of his pamphlets describing a Satanic ceremony and I believe this is worthy of inclusion. I must hasten to add that this is believed to be a *factual* description by Crowley of a ceremony he devised and performed himself several times. One would wish that it were only fiction. . . .

The Initiation

ALEISTER CROWLEY

In this ritual the initiate will crucify a toad with many a mocking curse. The catching of the frog must be done in silence.

The frog or toad being caught is kept all night in an ark or chest; and it is written 'Thou didst not abhor the Virgin's Womb.' Presently the frog will begin to leap therein, and this is an omen of good success. Dawn being come, thou shalt approach the chest with an offering of gold, and if available, of frankincense and of myrrh. Thou shalt then release the frog from the chest with many acts of homage and place it in apparent liberty. He may, for example, be placed on a quilt of many colours, and covered with a net.

Now take a vessel of water and approach the frog, saying: In the Name of the Father and of the Son and of the Holy Ghost (here sprinkle water on its head) I baptise thee, O creature of frogs, with water, by the name of Jesus of Nazareth.

During the day thou shalt approach the frog whenever convenient, and speak words of worship. And thou shalt ask it to perform such miracles as thou desirest to be done; and they shall be done according to Thy Will. Also thou shalt promise to the frog an elevation fitting him; and all this while thou shalt be secretly carving a cross whereon to crucify him.

Night being fallen, thou shalt arrest the frog and accuse him of blasphemy, sedition and so forth, in these words: Do what thou wilt shall be the whole of the Law.

Jesus of Nazareth, thou art taken in my snare. All my life

thou hast plagued me and affronted me. In thy name—with all other free souls in Christendom—I have been tortured in my boyhood; all delights have been forbidden unto me; all that I had has been taken from me, and that which is owed to me they pay not—in thy name. Now at last I have thee; the Slave-God is in the power of the Lord of Freedom. Thine hour is come; as I blot thee out from this earth, so surely shall the eclipse pass; and Light, Life, Love and Liberty be once more the Law of Earth. Give thy place to me, O Jesus; thine aeon is passed; the Age of Horus is arisen by the Magick of the Master the Great Beast that is Man; and his number is six hundred and three score and six.

I therefore condemn thee Jesus the slave-god to be mocked and spat upon and scourged, and then crucified.

This sentence is then executed. After the mocking upon the Cross, say thus: Do what thou wilt shall be the whole of the Law.

I, the Great Beast, slaying thee, Jesus of Nazareth the slave-god, under the form of this creature of frogs, do bless this creature in the name of the Father and of the Son and of the Holy Ghost. And I assume unto myself and take into my service the elemental spirit of this frog, to be about me as a lying spirit to go forth upon the earth as a guardian to me in my Work for Man; that men may speak of my piety and of my gentleness and of all virtues and bring to me love and service and all material things whatsoever I may stand in need. And this shall be its reward, to stand beside me and hear the truth that I utter, the falsehood whereof shall deceive men. Love is the law, love under will.

Then shalt thou stab the frog to the heart with the Dagger of Art, saying: Into my hands I receive thy spirit.

Presently thou shalt take down the frog from the cross and divide it into two parts; the legs shalt thou cook and eat as a sacrament to confirm thy compact with the frog; and the rest shalt thou burn utterly with fire, to consume finally the aeon of the accursed one. So it must be!

It would hardly be right not to include at least one story by a woman writer in this collection—though few of them seem to have tackled the subject during recent years. Whether this is just a lack of interest or nervousness where Satanism is concerned, I have been unable to ascertain. But of the stories by women which I have researched, 'The Book' by *Margaret Irwin* seems far and away the best. It is an atmospheric piece full of subtleties of plot and a splendid climax. Miss Irwin is a famous writer of historical novels and has had numerous best-sellers including *Royal Flush* and *The Gay Galliard*.

The Book

MARGARET IRWIN

On a foggy night in November, Mr. Corbett, having guessed the murderer by the third chapter of his detective story, arose in disappointment from his bed and went downstairs in search of something more satisfactory to send him to sleep.

The fog had crept through the closed and curtained windows of the dining-room and hung thick on the air, in a silence that seemed as heavy and breathless as the fog. The atmosphere was more choking than in his room, and very chill, although the remains of a large fire still burned in the grate.

The dining-room bookcase was the only considerable one in the house, and held a careless, unselected collection to suit all the tastes of the household, together with a few dull and obscure old theological books that had been left over from the sale of a learned uncle's library. Cheap red novels, bought on railway stalls by Mrs. Corbett, who thought a journey the only time to read, were thrust in like pert, undersized intruders among the respectable nineteenth-century works of culture, chastely bound in dark blue or green, which Mr. Corbett had considered the right thing to buy during his Oxford days; beside these there swaggered the children's large, gaily-bound story-books and collections of fairy tales in every colour.

From among this neat, new, cloth-bound crowd there towered here and there a musty sepulchre of learning, brown with the colour of dust rather than leather, with no trace of gilded letters, however faded, on its crumbling back to tell what lay inside. A few of these moribund survivors from the

Dean's library were inhospitably fastened with rusty clasps; all remained closed, and appeared impenetrable, their blank forbidding backs uplifted above their frivolous surroundings with the air of scorn that belongs to a private and concealed knowledge. For only the worm of corruption now bored his way through their evil-smelling pages.

It was an unusual flight of fancy for Mr. Corbett to imagine that the vaporous and fog-ridden air that seemed to hang more thickly about the bookcase was like a dank and poisonous breath exhaled by one or other of these slowly rotting volumes. Discomfort in this pervasive and impalpable presence came on him more acutely than at any time that day; in an attempt to clear his throat of it he choked most unpleasantly.

He hurriedly chose a Dickens from the second shelf as appropriate to a London fog, and had returned to the foot of the stairs when he decided that his reading tonight should by contrast be of blue Italian skies and white statues, in beautiful rhythmic sentences. He went back for a Walter Pater.

He found *Marius the Epicurean* tipped sideways across the gap left by his withdrawal of *The Old Curiosity Shop*. It was a very wide gap to have been left by a single volume, for the books on that shelf had been closely wedged together. He put the Dickens back into it and saw that there was still space for a large book. He said to himself in careful and precise words: 'This is nonsense. No one can possibly have gone into the dining-room and removed a book while I was crossing the hall. There must have been a gap before in the second shelf.' But another part of his mind kept saying in a hurried, tumbled torrent: 'There was no gap in the second shelf. There was no gap in the second shelf.'

He snatched at both the *Marius* and *The Old Curiosity Shop*, and went to his room in a haste that was unnecessary and absurd, since even if he believed in ghosts, which he did not, no one had the smallest reason for suspecting any in the modern Kensington house wherein he and his family had lived for the last fifteen years. Reading was the best thing to calm the nerves, and Dickens a pleasant, wholesome and robust author.

Tonight, however, Dickens struck him in a different light. Beneath the author's sentimental pity for the weak and helpless, he could discern a revolting pleasure in cruelty and suffering, while the grotesque figures of the people in Cruikshank's illustrations revealed too clearly the hideous distortions of their souls. What had seemed humorous now appeared diabolic, and in disgust at these two old favourites, he turned to Walter Pater for the repose and dignity of a classic spirit.

But presently he wondered if this spirit were not in itself of a marble quality, frigid and lifeless, contrary to the purpose of nature. 'I have often thought,' he said to himself, 'that there is something evil in the austere worship of beauty for its own sake.' He had never thought so before, but he liked to think that this impulse of fancy was the result of mature consideration, and with this satisfaction he composed himself for sleep.

He woke two or three times in the night, an unusual occurrence, but he was glad of it, for each time he had been dreaming horribly of these blameless Victorian works. Sprightly devils in whiskers and peg-top trousers tortured a lovely maiden and leered in delight at her anguish; the gods and heroes of classic fable acted deeds whose naked crime and shame Mr. Corbett had never appreciated in Latin and Greek Unseens. When he had woken in a cold sweat from the spectacle of the ravished Philomel's torn and bleeding tongue, he decided there was nothing for it but to go down and get another book that would turn his thoughts in some more pleasant direction. But his increasing reluctance to do this found a hundred excuses. The recollection of the gap in the shelf now recurred to him with a sense of unnatural importance; in the troubled dozes that followed, this gap between two books seemed the most hideous deformity, like a gap between the front teeth of some grinning monster.

But in the clear daylight of the morning Mr. Corbett came down to the pleasant dining-room, its sunny windows and smell of coffee and toast, and ate an undiminished breakfast with a mind chiefly occupied in self-congratulation that the wind had blown the fog away in time for his Saturday game of golf. Whistling happily, he was pouring out his final cup of coffee, when his hand remained arrested in the act as his glance, roving across to the bookcase, noticed that there was now no gap at all in the second shelf. He asked who had been at the bookcase already, but neither of the girls had, nor Dicky, and Mrs. Corbett was not yet down. The maid never touched the books. They wanted to know what book he missed in it, which made him look foolish, as he could not say. The things that disturb us at midnight are negligible at 9 a.m.

'I thought there was a gap in the second shelf,' he said, 'but it doesn't matter.'

'There never is a gap in the second shelf,' said little Jean brightly. 'You can take out lots of books from it and when you go back the gap's always filled up. Haven't you noticed that? I have.'

Nora, the middle one in age, said Jean was always being silly; she had been found crying over the funny pictures in the *Rose and the Ring* because she said all the people in them had such wicked faces, and the picture of a black cat had upset her because she thought it was a witch. Mr. Corbett did not like to think of such fancies for his Jeannie. She retaliated briskly by saying Dicky was just as bad and he was a big boy. He had kicked a book across the room and said: 'Filthy stuff,' just like that. Jean was a good mimic; her tone expressed a venom of disgust, and she made the gesture of dropping a book as though the very touch of it were loathsome. Dicky, who had been making violent signs at her, now told her she was a beastly little sneak and he would never again take her for rides on the step of his bicycle. Mr. Corbett was disturbed. Unpleasant housemaids and bad school-friends passed through his head, as he gravely asked his son how he had got hold of this book.

'Took it out of that bookcase, of course,' said Dicky furiously.

It turned out to be the *Boy's Gulliver's Travels* that granny had given him, and Dicky had at last to explain his rage with the devil who wrote it to show that men were worse than beasts and the human race a wash-out. A boy who never had good school reports had no right to be so morbidly sensitive as to penetrate to the underlying cycnicism of Swift's delightful fable, and that moreover in the bright and carefully expurgated edition they bring out nowadays. Mr. Corbett could not say he had ever noticed the cynicism himself, though he knew from the critical books it must be there, and with some annoyance he advised his son to take out a nice, bright, modern boy's adventure story that could not depress anybody. It appeared, however, that Dicky was 'off reading just now', and the girls echoed this.

Mr. Corbett soon found that he too was 'off reading'. Every new book seemed to him weak, tasteless and insipid; while his old and familiar books were depressing or even, in some obscure way, disgusting. Authors must all be filthy-minded; they probably wrote what they dared not express in their lives. Stevenson had said that literature was a morbid secretion; he read Stevenson again to discover his peculiar morbidity, and detected in his essays a self-pity masquerading as courage, and in *Treasure Island* an invalid's sickly attraction to brutality.

This gave him a zest to find out what he disliked so much, and his taste for reading revived as he explored with relish the hidden infirmities of minds that had been valued by fools as great and noble. He saw Jane Austen and Charlotte Brontë as two unpleasant examples of spinsterhood; the one as a prying, sub-acid busybody in everyone else's flirtations, the other as a raving, craving mænad seeking self-immolation on the altar of her frustrated passions. He compared Wordsworth's love of nature to the monstrous egoism of an ancient bell-wether, isolated from the flock.

These powers of penetration astonished him. With a mind so acute and original he should have achieved greatness, yet he was a mere solicitor, and not prosperous at that. If he had but the money, he might do something with those ivory shares, but it would be a pure gamble and he had no luck. His natural envy of his wealthier acquaintance now mingled with a contempt for their stupidity that approached loathing. The digestion of his lunch in the City was ruined by meeting sentimental yet successful dotards whom he had once regarded as pleasant fellows. The very sight of them spoiled his game of golf, so that he came to prefer reading alone in the dining-room even on sunny afternoons.

He discovered also and with a slight shock that Mrs. Corbett had always bored him. Dicky he began actively to dislike as an impudent blockhead, and the two girls were as insipidly alike as white mice; it was a relief when he abolished their tiresome habit of coming in to say good night.

In the now unbroken silence and seclusion of the dining-room, he read with feverish haste as though he were seeking for some clue to knowledge, some secret key to existence which would quicken and inflame it, transform it from its present dull torpor to a life worthy of him and his powers.

He even explored the few decaying remains of his uncle's theological library. Bored and baffled, he yet persisted, and had the occasional relief of an ugly woodcut of Adam and Eve with figures like bolsters and hair like dahlias, or a map of the Cosmos with Hell-mouth in the corner, belching forth demons. One of these books had diagrams and symbols in the margin which he took to be mathematical formulæ of a kind he did not know. He presently discovered that they were drawn, not printed, and that the book was in manuscript, in a very neat, crabbed black writing that resembled black-letter printing. It was, moreover, in Latin, a fact that gave Mr. Corbett a shock of unreasoning disappointment. For while examining the signs in the margin, he had been filled with an extraordinary exultation, as though he knew himself to be on the edge of a discovery that should alter his whole life. But he had forgotten his Latin.

With a secret and guilty air which would have looked absurd to anyone who knew his harmless purpose, he stole to the schoolroom for Dicky's Latin dictionary and grammar, and hurried back to the dining-room, where he tried to discover what the book was about with an anxious industry that surprised himself. There was no name to it, nor of the author. Several blank pages had been left at the end, and the writing ended at the bottom of a page, with no flourish or superscription, as though the book had been left unfinished. From what sentences he could translate, it seemed to be a work on theology rather than mathematics. There were constant references to the Master, to His wishes and injunctions, which appeared to be of a complicated kind. Mr. Corbett began by skipping these as mere accounts of ceremonial, but a word caught his eye as one unlikely to occur in such an account. He read this passage attentively, looking up each word in the dictionary, and could hardly believe the result of his translation. 'Clearly,' he decided, 'this book must be by some early missionary, and the passage I have just read the account of some horrible rite practised by a savage tribe of devil-worshippers.' Though he called it 'horrible', he reflected on it, committing each detail to memory. He then amused himself by copying the signs in the margin near it and trying to discover their significance. But a sensation of sickly cold came over him, his head swam, and he could hardly see the figures before his eyes. He suspected a sudden attack of influenza, and went to ask his wife for medicine.

They were all in the drawing-room, Mrs. Corbett helping Nora and Jean with a new game, Dicky playing the pianola, and Mike, the Irish terrier, who had lately deserted his accustomed place on the dining-room hearthrug, stretched by the fire. Mr. Corbett had an instant's impression of this peaceful and cheerful scene, before his family turned towards him and asked in scared tones what was the matter. He thought how like sheep they looked and sounded; nothing in his appearance in the mirror struck him as odd; it was their gaping faces that were unfamiliar. He then noticed the extraordinary behaviour of Mike, who had sprung from the hearthrug and was crouched in the farthest corner, uttering no sound, but with his eyes distended and foam round his bared teeth. Under Mr. Corbett's glance he slunk towards the door, whimpering in a faint and abject manner, and then, as his master called him, he snarled horribly, and the hair bristled on the scruff of his neck. Dicky let him out, and they heard him scuffling at a frantic rate down the stairs to the kitchen, and then, again and again, a long-drawn howl.

'What *can* be the matter with Mike?' asked Mrs. Corbett.

Her question broke a silence that seemed to have lasted a long time. Jean began to cry. Mr. Corbett said irritably that he did not know what was the matter with any of them.

Then Nora asked, 'What is that red mark on your face?'

He looked again in the glass and could see nothing.

'It's quite clear from here,' said Dicky; 'I can see the lines in the finger-print.'

'Yes, that's what it is,' said Mrs. Corbett in her brisk, staccato voice; 'the print of a finger on your forehead. Have you been writing in red ink?'

Mr. Corbett precipitately left the room for his own, where he sent down a message that he was suffering from headache and would have his dinner in bed. He wanted no one fussing round him. By next morning he was amazed at his fancies of influenza, for he had never felt so well in his life.

No one commented on his looks at breakfast, so he concluded that the mark had disappeared. The old Latin book he had been translating on the previous night had been moved from the writing bureau, although Dicky's grammar and dictionary were still there. The second shelf was, as always in the daytime, closely packed; the book had, he remembered, been in the second shelf. But this time he did not ask who had put it back.

That day he had an unexpected stroke of luck in a new client of the name of Crab, who entrusted him with large sums of money: nor was he irritated by the sight of his more prosperous acquaintance, but with difficulty refrained from grinning in their faces, so confident was he that his remarkable ability must soon place him higher than any of them. At dinner he chaffed his family with what he felt to be the gaiety of a schoolboy. But on them it had a contrary effect, for they stared, either at him in stupid astonishment, or at their plates, depressed and nervous. Did they think him drunk? he wondered, and a fury came on him at their low and bestial suspicions and heavy dullness of mind. Why, he was younger than any of them.

But in spite of this new alertness, he could not attend to the letters he should have written that evening, and drifted to the bookcase for a little light distraction, but found that for the first time there was nothing he wished to read. He pulled out a book from above his head at random, and saw that it was the old Latin book in manuscript. As he turned over its stiff and yellow pages, he noticed with pleasure the smell of corruption that had first repelled him in these decaying volumes, a smell, he now thought, of ancient and secret knowledge.

This idea of secrecy seemed to affect him personally, for on hearing a step in the hall he hastily closed the book and put it back in its place. He went to the schoolroom where Dicky was doing his homework, and told him he required his Latin grammar and dictionary again for an old law report. To his annoyance he stammered and put his words awkwardly; he thought that the boy looked oddly at him and he cursed him in his heart for a suspicious young devil, though of what he should be suspicious he could not say. Nevertheless, when back in the dining-room, he listened at the door and then softly turned the lock before he opened the books on the writing bureau.

The script and Latin seemed much clearer than on the previous evening, and he was able to read at random a passage relating to the trial of a German midwife in 1620 for the murder and dissection of 783 children. Even allowing for the opportunties afforded by her profession, the number appeared excessive, nor could he discover any motive for the slaughter.

He decided to translate the book from the beginning.

It appeared to be an account of some secret society whose activities and ritual were of a nature so obscure, and when not, so vile and terrible, that Mr. Corbett would not at first believe that this could be a record of any human mind, although his deep interest in it should have convinced him that from his humanity, at least, it was not altogether alien.

He read until far later than his usual hour for bed, and when at last he rose, it was with the book in his hands. To defer his parting with it, he stood turning over the pages until he reached the end of the writing, and was struck by a new peculiarity.

The ink was much fresher and of a far poorer quality than the thick, rusted ink in the bulk of the book; on close inspection he would have said that it was of modern manufacture and written quite recently, were it not for the fact that it was in the same crabbed, late seventeenth-century handwriting.

This, however, did not explain the perplexity, even dismay and fear, he now felt as he stared at the last sentence. It ran: 'Contine te in perennibus studiis', and he had at once recognised it as a Ciceronian tag that had been dinned into him at school. He could not understand how he had failed to notice it yesterday.

Then he remembered that the book had ended at the bottom of a page. But now the last two sentences were written at the very top of a page. However long he looked at them, he could come to no other conclusion than that they had been added since the previous evening.

He now read the sentence before the last: 'Re imperfecta mortuus sum', and translated the whole as: 'I died with my purpose unachieved. Continue, thou, the never-ending studies.'

With his eyes still fixed upon it, Mr. Corbett replaced the book on the writing bureau and stepped back from it to the door, his hand outstretched behind him, groping and then tugging at the door-handle. As the door failed to open, his breath came in a faint, hardly articulate scream. Then he remembered that he had himself locked it, and he fumbled with the key in frantic, ineffectual movements until at last he opened it and banged it after him as he plunged backwards into the hall.

For a moment he stood there looking at the door-handle; then with a stealthy, sneaking movement, his hand crept out towards it, touched it, began to turn it, when suddenly he pulled his hand away and went up to his bedroom, three steps at a time.

There he behaved in a manner only comparable with the way he had lost his head after losing his innocence when a schoolboy of sixteen. He hid his face in the pillow, he cried, he raved in meaningless words, repeating: 'Never, never, never. I will never do it again. Help me never to do it again.' With the words 'Help me,' he noticed what he was saying, they reminded him of other words, and he began to pray aloud. But the words sounded jumbled, they persisted in coming into his head in a reverse order, so that he found he was saying his prayers backwards, and at this final absurdity he suddenly began to laugh very loud. He sat up on the bed, delighted at this return to sanity, common sense and humour, when the door leading into Mrs. Corbett's room opened, and he saw his wife staring at him with a strange, grey, drawn face that made her seem like the terror-stricken ghost of her usually smug and placid self.

'It's not burglars,' he said irritably. 'I've come to bed late, that is all, and must have waked you.'

'Henry,' said Mrs. Corbett, and he noticed that she had not heard him. 'Henry, didn't you hear it?'

'What?'

'That laugh.'

He was silent, an instinctive caution warning him to wait until she spoke again. And this she did, imploring him with her eyes to reassure her.

'It was not a human laugh. It was like the laugh of a devil.'

He checked his violent inclination to laugh again. It was wiser not to let her know that it was only his laughter she had heard. He told her to stop being fanciful, and Mrs. Corbett, gradually recovering her docility, returned to obey an impossible command, since she could not stop being what she had never been.

The next morning, Mr. Corbett rose before any of the servants and crept down to the dining-room. As before, the dictionary and grammar alone remained on the writing bureau; the book was back on the second shelf. He opened it at the end. Two more lines had been added, carrying the writing down to the middle of the page. They ran:

Ex auro canceris
In dentem elephantis,

which he translated as:

Out of the money of the crab
Into the tooth of the elephant.

From this time on, his acquaintance in the City noticed a change in the mediocre, rather flabby and unenterprising 'old Corbett'. His recent sour depression dropped from him: he seemed to have grown twenty years younger, strong, brisk and cheerful, and with a self-confidence in business that struck them as lunacy. They waited with a not unpleasant excitement for the inevitable crash, but his every speculation, however wild and hare-brained, turned out successful. He no longer avoided them, but went out of his way to display his consciousness of luck, daring and vigour, and to chaff them in a manner that began to make him actively disliked. This he welcomed with delight as a sign of others' envy and his superiority.

He never stayed in town for dinners or theatres, for he was always now in a hurry to get home, where, as soon as he was sure of being undisturbed, he would take down the manuscript book from the second shelf of the dining-room and turn to the last pages.

Every morning he found that a few words had been added since the evening before, and always they formed, as he considered, injunctions to himself. These were at first only with regard to his money transactions, giving assurance to his boldest fancies, and since the brilliant and unforeseen success that had attended his gamble with Mr. Crab's money in African ivory, he followed all such advice unhesitatingly.

But presently, interspersed with these commands, were others of a meaningless, childish, yet revolting character, such as might be invented by a decadent imbecile, or, it must be admitted, by the idle fancies of any ordinary man who permits his imagination to wander unbridled. Mr. Corbett was startled to recognise one or two such fancies of his own, which had occurred to him during his frequent boredom in church, and which he had not thought any other mind could conceive.

He at first paid no attention to these directions, but found that his new speculations declined so rapidly that he became terrified not merely for his fortune but for his reputation and even safety, since the money of various of his clients was involved. It was made clear to him that he must follow the commands in the book altogether or not at all, and he began to carry out their puerile and grotesque blasphemies with a contemptuous amusement, which, however, gradually changed to a sense of their monstrous significance. They became more capricious and difficult of execution, but he now never hesitated to obey blindly, urged by a fear that he could not understand, but knew only that it was not of mere financial failure.

By now he understood the effect of this book on the others near it, and the reason that had impelled its mysterious agent to move the books into the second shelf so that all in turn should come under the influence of that ancient and secret knowledge.

In respect to it, he encouraged his children, with jeers at their stupidity, to read more, but he could not observe that they ever now took a book from the dining-room bookcase. He himself no longer needed to read, but went to bed early and slept sound. The things that all his life he had longed to do when he should have enough money now seemed to him insipid. His most exciting pleasure was the smell and touch of these mouldering pages, as he turned them to find the last message inscribed to him.

One evening it was in two words only: 'Canem occide.'

He laughed at this simple and pleasant request to kill the dog, for he bore Mike a grudge for his change from devotion to slinking aversion. Moreover, it could not have come more opportunely, since in turning out an old desk he had just discovered some packets of rat poison bought years ago and forgotten. No one therefore knew of its existence, and it would be easy to poison Mike without any further suspicion than that of a neighbour's carelessness. He whistled lightheartedly as he ran upstairs to rummage for the packets, and returned to empty one in the dog's dish of water in the hall.

That night the household was awakened by terrified screams proceeding from the stairs. Mr. Corbett was the first to hasten there, prompted by the instinctive caution that was always with him these days. He saw Jean, in her nightdress, scrambling up on to the landing on her hands and knees, clutching at anything that afforded support and screaming in a choking, tearless, unnatural manner. He carried her to the room she shared with Nora, where they were quickly followed by Mrs. Corbett.

Nothing coherent could be got from Jean. Nora said that she must have been having her old dream again; when her father demanded what this was, she said that Jean sometimes woke in the night, crying, because she had dreamed of a hand passing backwards and forwards over the dining-room bookcase, until it found a certain book and took it out of the shelf. At this point she was always so frightened that she woke up.

On hearing this, Jean broke into fresh screams, and Mrs. Corbett would have no more explanations. Mr. Corbett went out on to the stairs to find what had brought the child there from her bed. On looking down into the lighted hall, he saw Mike's dish overturned. He went down to examine it and saw that the water he had poisoned must have been upset and absorbed by the rough doormat, which was quite wet.

He went back to the little girls' room, told his wife that she was tired and must go to bed, and he would take his turn at comforting Jean. She was now much quieter. He took her on his knee, where at first she shrank from him. Mr. Corbett remembered with an angry sense of injury that she never now sat on his knee, and would have liked to pay her out for it by mocking and frightening her. But he had to coax her into telling what he wanted, and with this object he soothed her, calling her by pet names that he thought he had forgotten, telling her that nothing could hurt her now he was with her.

At first his cleverness amused him; he chuckled softly when Jean buried her head in his dressing-gown. But presently an uncomfortable sensation came over him, he gripped at Jean as though for her protection, while he was so smoothly assuring her of his. With difficulty he listened to what he had at last induced her to tell him.

She and Nora had kept Mike with them all the evening and taken him to sleep in their room for a treat. He had lain at the foot of Jean's bed and they had all gone to sleep. Then Jean began her old dream of the hand moving over the books in the dining-room bookcase; but instead of taking out a book, it came across the dining-room and out on to the stairs. It came up over the banisters and to the door of their room, and turned their door-handle very softly and opened it. At this point she jumped up wide awake and turned on the light, calling to Nora. The door which had been shut when they went to sleep, was wide open, and Mike was gone.

She told Nora that she was sure something dreadful would happen to him if she did not go and bring him back, and ran down into the hall, where she saw him just about to drink from his dish. She called to him and he looked up, but did not come, so she ran to him and began to pull him along with her, when her nightdress was clutched from behind and then she felt a hand seize her arm.

She fell down, and then clambered upstairs as fast as she

could, screaming all the way.

It was now clear to Mr. Corbett that Mike's dish must have been upset in the scuffle. She was again crying, but this time he felt himself unable to comfort her. He retired to his room, where he walked up and down in an agitation he could not understand, for he found his thoughts perpetually arguing on a point that had never troubled him before.

'I am not a bad man,' he kept saying to himself. 'I have never done anything actually wrong. My clients are none the worse for my speculations, only the better. Nor have I spent my new wealth on gross and sensual pleasures; these now have even no attraction for me.'

Presently he added: 'It is not wrong to try and kill a dog, an ill-tempered brute. It turned against me. It might have bitten Jeannie.'

He noticed that he had thought of her as Jeannie, which he had not done for some time; it must have been because he had called her that tonight. He must forbid her ever to leave her room at night, he could not have her meddling. It would be safer for him if she were not there at all.

Again that sick and cold sensation of fear swept over him: he seized the bed-post as though he were falling, and held on to it for some minutes. 'I was thinking of a boarding school,' he told himself, and then, 'I must go down and find out—find out——' He would not think what it was he must find out.

He opened his door and listened. The house was quiet. He crept on to the landing and along to Nora's and Jean's door, where again he stood listening. There was no sound, and at that he was again overcome with unreasonable terror. He imagined Jean lying very still in her bed—too still. He hastened away from the door, shuffling in his bedroom slippers along the passage and down the stairs.

A bright fire still burned in the dining-room grate. A glance at the clock told him it was not yet twelve. He stared at the bookcase. In the second shelf was a gap which had not been there when he had left. On the writing bureau lay a large open book. He knew that he must cross the room and see what was written in it. Then, as before, words that he did not intend came sobbing and crying to his lips, muttering: 'No, no, not that. Never, never, never.' But he crossed the room and looked down at the book. As last time, the message was in only two words: 'Infantem occide.'

He slipped and fell forward against the bureau. His hands clutched at the book, liften it as he recovered himself, and with his finger he traced out the words that had been written. The smell of corruption crept into his nostrils. He told himself that he was not a snivelling dotard, but a man stronger and wiser than his fellows, superior to the common emotions of humanity, who held in his hands the sources of ancient and secret power.

He had known what the message would be. It was after all the only safe and logical thing to do. Jean had acquired dangerous knowledge. She was a spy, an antagonist. That she was so unconsciously, that she was eight years old, his youngest and favourite child, were sentimental appeals that could make no difference to a man of sane reasoning power such as his own. Jean had sided with Mike against him. 'All that are not with me are against me,' he repeated softly. He would kill both dog and child with the white powder that no one knew to be in his possession. It would be quite safe.

He laid down the book and went to the door. What he had to do he would do quickly, for again that sensation of deadly cold was sweeping over him. He wished he had not to do it tonight; last night it would have been easier, but tonight she had sat on his knee and made him afraid. He imagined her lying very still in her bed—too still. But it would be she who would lie there, not he, so why should he be afraid? He was protected by ancient and secret powers. He held on to the door-handle, but his fingers seemed to have grown numb, for he could not turn it. He clung to it, crouched and shivering, bending over it until he knelt on the ground, his head beneath the handle which he still clutched with upraised hands. Suddenly the hands were loosened and flung outwards with the frantic gesture of a man falling from a great height, and he stumbled to his feet. He seized the book and threw it on the fire. A violent sensation of choking overcame him, he felt he was being strangled, as in a nightmare he tried again and again to shriek aloud, but his breath would make no sound. His breath would not come at all. He fell backwards heavily, down on the floor, where he lay very still.

In the morning the maid who came to open the dining-room windows found her master dead. The sensation caused by this was scarcely so great in the City as that given by the simultaneous collapse of all Mr. Corbett's recent speculations. It was instantly assumed that he must have had previous knowledge of this and so committed suicide.

The stumbling-block of this theory was that the medical report defined the cause of Mr. Corbett's death as strangulation of the wind-pipe by the pressure of a hand which had left the marks of its fingers on his throat.

If any reader is still dismissing every story he reads as pure fiction, the invention of fertile minds, with no actual basis in reality, he is warned to treat this next item with great care. It is certainly one of the most impressive—and chilling—stories I read during my extensive researches in both England and America for this book. Of the author, *Cleve Cartmill*, we know very little. A retiring man who shuns publicity, he was relatively productive for a number of years just after the war and then virtually disappeared into limbo. He has not written a new story for several years now, despite continuing requests by readers in the American magazine he once contributed to. I will offer no clues about the contents of 'No News Today'. You are on your own from here. . . .

No News Today

CLEVE CARTMILL

Some of you will be disappointed because this editorial completely fills today's issue of the *Argus*. But I feel it is more important than news, this article. And some of the stores may be annoyed because there is no room for their ads, but a newspaper's first duty is to its readers.

You will not see me any more, so I take this means to impress on your minds one fact:

Dr. Evan Scot is not a son of Satan.

You must believe that. I am going to give you the reasons, and you will see. Then, when I finish, and after Mother Grace has run off enough copies for our subscribers, we will clean up the press, have a couple of drinks, and step through the door into the black emptiness which has been there for three days, blotting all lights, waiting for us.

I'll tell you about that blackness in due time. First, I want to explain that the rumour about Dr. Scot would never have been started if Mother Grace had attended to his job.

That was last week, the day after graduation exercises at the high school. Mother Grace came into my office from the composing room and flung several sheets of copy on my desk.

'I'll s-set no copy for a s-son of Satan,' he said. He stutters a little when he is excited.

I put my feet down and looked at the copy. It was an account of the exercises, and included a few excerpts from Dr. Scot's commencement address. I then looked at Mother Grace.

He was a pink ball of indignation, his white hair almost standing out straight, his blue eyes flickering, and his round chin out-thrust like a shelf.

I didn't say anything. I simply went out to the composing room and took a look at the jug of whisky that caused Judith to name him 'Mother'. She said he cradled it like a lost child on Saturday nights. The jug was untouched, as it had been for the last month, since Mother went on the wagon because of the research which engaged his free time.

Back in my office, I frowned down at him. 'What's it all about, Mother?'

'Evan Scot is the spawn of Lucifer. I'm damned if I'll set any type that's got his name in it.'

'Dr. Scot is one of our most prominent citizens.'

'That's what I mean, Buck.'

'You're not making sense. Explain yourself.'

'I don't dare, Buck. I like you. Just edit Scot's name out of the story and we'll forget the matter.'

'We can't leave Scot's name out of the story. He was one of the highlights. The school board would be on our necks. So would Judith. She'd want to know why we messed up her copy. What would you tell her?'

'I wouldn't tell her anything, Buck. Same as I won't tell you.'

I didn't want to fire him. He's a good printer. He's been all over the world several times, has worked in every State in the Union, and he treats a Linotype like a younger brother. He had settled here in my shop two years ago, and was as much a part of the place as the weathered 'Job Printing' sign over the door. No, I didn't want to fire him, but I had to have some kind of discipline.

'Set the story as it is,' I said.

'S-set it yourself. I'm q-quitting.'

He took off his apron, put on his coat, and stamped out with a thirsty gleam in his eye.

Many of you know what that little man did. He got drunk

and started the rumour about Dr. Scot. I don't think anybody paid any attention to him except Ralph Lake, but we took care of Ralph last night. I'm sure he doesn't believe it any longer, and he'll never see this editorial.

While Mother was getting drunk, I knew nothing about it, of course. I was busy setting type. I'm not too good at it, as you will remember. That was the issue which carried Henry Longernin's name misspelled six ways, and in which the PTA story did not appear. That was the issue which carried so many short paragraphs of odd facts about different parts of the world. Such paragraphs are kept standing on galleys in any print shop to use as filler, and I was too slow on the Linotype to set all the local copy Judith had turned in, so I threw in several columns of filler.

When I was making up the pages, I was reminded of the predicament another country editor got into when he ran short of filler one day. His paper was full, except for a couple of inches in one lower corner of his front page. He was one of those crusading, bitter cusses that gave so much colour to early American frontiers, and he set up a paragraph by hand in large type so that it would fill the hole. The paragraph: 'A local banker and another rat fought with their fists last night at the corner of First and Main until a gentleman who was asleep in the gutter woke up and asked them to be more quiet.' All three of the men referred to took a poke at the editor next day, and it is said that the practice of keeping fillers on hand started at that time.

At any rate, I had plenty, and when I had run off the edition on the flatbed press I went home to bed. I didn't know what had happened to Mother, and I knew I would need another printer.

I got some inkling of Mother's activities the next morning when Dr. Evan Scot stalked into my office. He gave me a nod of cold recognition, and refused to take a chair.

'I have come to demand an apology, Mr. Buck.'

This was not the hearty, pompous Dr. Scot I knew. He had

an icy purpose in his eyes, and his chubby hands were rigid. I picked up a copy of the *Argus*, and skimmed through the commencement story which I had set.

'Are you misquoted, doctor? Name spelled wrong?'

He waved an impatient white hand. 'I don't know, I haven't even glanced at your paper. An employee of yours, I am told, a man named Grace, has slandered me.'

'He's no longer an employee of mine.'

Dr. Scot inclined his head in a fractional bow. 'Very well, I shall take the matter up with the—ah, proper authorities. Sorry to have disturbed you, Mr. Buck.'

As he turned to go, feet scuffed across the reception room, and Mother Grace came to the door, stood swaying a little on widespread legs. He was drunk.

'Your evilness,' he saluted Dr. Scot.

The doctor gave Mother an aloof examination, eyes lit by a remote curiosity as they touched on Mother's puffed face, tousled white hair, wrinkled clothes, and stubbly beard.

'You talk too much,' Dr. Scot said.

'But with authority, sir,' Mother replied.

'What authority?'

'The very highest, I suspect. The "Sabbaticon".'

'What is that?'

Mother Grace leered crookedly. 'Don't play innocent, prince.'

Dr. Scot's reaction to this was what caused me to agree with Mother Grace until Satan's public-relations counsel set us straight on the matter. Dr. Scot was angry. You could see a muscle twitch under one jowl, and his ample shoulders lifted a fraction. But his anger was cold. Thoughtful is perhaps a better term. He held his gaze steady on Mother Grace for a full ten seconds. Then:

'You talk too much,' he repeated, and thrust through the door.

Mother Grace stared after him for a few seconds, then came

inside unsteadily and dropped into a chair.

'Buck, I want to talk to you.'

'You'd better. What goes on, Mother? Are you serious in this talk about Dr. Scot?'

'Deadly, Buck. And I've got a notion that it *is* deadly, too. I don't think I'll be around much longer. But before I disappear, I'd like to get some information out to the public.'

'Disappear to where?'

'Who knows? Where did the others disappear to? The ones who walked through their doors and were never seen again? I don't know where they went, but I think I know why. Do you want to hear about it?'

'If it's entertaining, and brief.'

'It may be dangerous, Buck.'

'Nonsense. You're still drunk.'

Mother looked at me with a still, unwavering earnestness. 'Yes, I am, a little. Otherwise I'd be afraid to tell you. But I can't keep it bottled up any longer. Wait.'

He went into the composing room, and I could hear him rummaging in the little cubbyhole where he slept. He came back with a peculiar book and several pages of manuscript in his careful handwriting. He tossed the book on my desk.

'That's the "Sabbaticon", Buck.'

It seemed to be of leather. The cover was a heavy sort of calf, with no inscription or decoration, and the pages were of a thin, almost transparent leather, with a texture like heavy crêpe. These pages were closely covered with symbols which were strange to me. I had never seen a language with characters remotely similar.

I laid the book aside. 'Well?'

'That's the handbook for the Sons of Satan.'

'Let's have it from the beginning, Mother. You're still not making sense.'

He began to talk, and after a few minutes I went through the reception room and locked the front door. I didn't want us to be interrupted.

He said that, according to this all-leather book, a world-wide society, called the Sons of Satan, had been formed early in the history of civilisation. The title of the group is accurate, he said; they are physical offspring of the devil, conceived in unions at Sabbats, gatherings of worshippers of evil.

'Where did you get this book?' I asked.

Mother Grace gave me a bleak look. 'It belonged to my mother, Buck.'

'Good heavens. What does that mean?'

'I don't know. I don't want to know. She died when I was born, and my uncle who raised and educated me gave it to me among other effects she had left. I've spent my life trying to translate it. The language isn't Latin, Greek, Sanskrit, or any other known today. I finished the translation a couple of weeks ago.'

'How do you know your translation is correct?'

'I . . . I feel it, Buck. Here's the meat of it, the rules of operation.' He handed me part of his translation.

I won't reproduce it here. There isn't space, nor time, perhaps. We're a little rushed for time. We're getting hungry, and we are determined not to suffer. We are just going to step through the door into that dead-black void.

But the rules. The Sons of Satan are supposed to be men of comfortable means. No more. Not wealthy, but the kind we common work-a-day folk admire. The men who are active in community affairs, the kind who are pointed out as local examples for children to follow.

They are not many, these Sons of Satan; only enough to provide a flavour of moderate success everywhere.

Their opinions are respected, but of course, divided. Thus they attract followers to both sides of any question. This stirs up conflict that is highly desirable from their point of view. Their principal advice to youth is roughly: 'Work. Earn your bread by the sweat of your brow. Keep your nose to the grindstone. Fame and success can be yours only if you are diligent.'

'Making a virtue of a curse on mankind,' Mother Grace commented on this.

'Diligence is a virtue,' I said. 'Men do succeed by constant effort.'

'How many?' Mother Grace jeered. 'What percentage of those who slave away their lives ever attain to comfort? I'll tell you. Only enough to promote envy, dissatisfaction, and uneasiness. It's in there. Read on.'

I see that in describing the text of the 'Sabbaticon' I have written in the present indicative. 'They are,' I have said of the Sons of Satan. I want to make it clear that I don't believe they exist. You must not believe it, either.

I finished. I looked at Mother Grace. 'I don't believe it.'

He picked up the leather book and opened it to the last page. 'It's easy to check. All I have to do is read a paragraph aloud. If my translation is correct, we'll have the old boy himself here in the office.'

'Don't be idiotic.'

'Want me to try? Want me to summon up the Prince of Darkness? I've been afraid to try before.'

'Your translation may be correct, but the whole book is probably a prehistoric fairy tale.'

'By whom, Buck? By whom?'

'How should I know?' The uneasy feeling I'd had while reading his translation began to wear off, and I managed a grin. 'Go ahead. Give him a call. We'll get an exclusive interview.'

Mother Grace stacked the sheets of his translation neatly on one corner of my desk, pushed his chair to one side, and knelt. Despite his rumpled condition and appearance of hard wear, he had a curious dignity.

'I hope we know what I'm doing,' he said softly, and began to chant in a monotone.

He had hardly said two words, or phrases, or whatever, of that scrambled language before we had a visitor.

He appeared in the connecting doorway to the reception room. Appeared suddenly, silently, without any traditional puffs of smoke or smell of brimstone. He was young, and aside from his somewhat peculiar ears and odd black costume, he was not very different from the rest of us.

He broke into Mother Grace's chant. 'You talk too much.' He pointed a long, dark finger at the 'Sabbaticon', said, 'You have no right to that,' and the book vanished. 'Or that,' he said, and the translation was gone.

'Shut up!' he said as Mother Grace opened his mouth as if to ask a question. 'Listen to me, both of you. I am going to leave you here. Any time you like, just step out of a door, or window, and you'll receive detailed attention.'

He seemed about to leave. 'May I ask a question?'

He flicked an impatient look at me. 'What do you want?'

'You mentioned detailed attention. What does that mean?'

'You'll see.'

'Are you Satan himself?' Mother Grace asked.

'Certainly not,' the creature snapped. 'He has better matters to occupy him. I'm his public-relations counsel.'

'B-but the invocation,' Mother stuttered. 'It was s-supposed to call up the d-devil.'

The creature looked at Mother Grace long and thoughtfully. 'So that's what you were doing? I—see. I'll be back,' he said, and vanished.

Mother Grace got up off his knees. He was trembling. But no more than I was. The full impact of the event had just hit me. We looked at each other and worked our mouths in an effort to speak, but couldn't make a sound. Mother Grace staggered to the door.

Something brought him up short. Nothing physical, but something he saw. He looked fixedly toward the street for some time. He found his voice, or at least a ghost of it.

'C-come here, B-Buck.'

That was when I saw the darkness.

I couldn't see through the windows or the glass on the door.

I could hear traffic sounds in the street as usual, but I couldn't see anything. The word 'ARGUS' on the big window was clearly outlined on the deeper black beyond.

I didn't feel that somebody had painted the windows. I felt that the dark had existence, beyond the windows and the door. I felt that it had—well, entity. I feel that way now, while I'm writing this.

I had a bad time getting out the words: 'Open the door, Mother, open the door.'

He went to the door, unlocked it, yanked it open. He shrank back, and I, even though I was across the room, took a backward step.

We couldn't see through the open door.

It's hard to tell about that darkness. If I try, I'll make it sound ridiculous. So I'd better not try. Just take my word for it, it wasn't at all ridiculous.

Somebody called from outside: 'Hello, Buck. Hello, Mother.'

We each lifted a hand. As we did so, Judith stepped through that black nothingness, her hair an almost blinding brightness against the background, and the white silhouette of her dress was like a cutout pattern.

We stood for a moment, Mother examining the floor, I trying to see some flicker of movement in traffic I could hear outside, Judith examining both of us. I knew suddenly I had to know what would happen if I stepped outside. I had to know if we had been tricked. I took a pencil from my pocket.

'Here,' I said to Judith. 'Toss this through the door.'

She frowned. 'Games?'

'Just throw it.'

She did so, and I heard it fall on the walk. It hit that curtain of blackness and, for me, vanished. 'Now bring it to me, please.'

'I'm no water spaniel,' she said. 'Fetch it yourself.'

'I mean it, Judith. This is no gag.'

She shook a puzzled head and stepped into nothing. She

came back and gave me the pencil. I threw it.

I didn't hear it fall.

Judith blinked. 'You ought to go on the stage, Buck. I saw it, then I didn't. Nice illusion.'

'Little thing I picked up,' I said.

'From your tone, I'd say you dug it up.'

'What did you see, chicken?'

'See? I know enough about that sort of thing to know I didn't *see* anything. I thought, though, I saw a pencil fly barely through the door and—*f-f-ft*. It wasn't there any more. How did you do it?'

'It's a secret.' To Mother Grace, who was staring at the door, I said, 'Let's go to work.'

He ambled into the composing room. I flung another look at the door and started after him.

'Buck,' Judith said softly, 'wait a minute.'

She looked unhappy, puzzled. 'What is it, kid?'

'It's about Ralph, Buck. And what Mother Grace told him last night.'

'Come in my office.' When we were in there, and I couldn't see the blackness, 'Tell,' I said.

'Well, Mother got stiff as a butler last night and gave Ralph a lot of guff about how we're being tricked by some crazy devil's club, he calls it. He was so convincing that Ralph believes it. So Ralph wants to ring wedding bells, even though we're broke. The hell with work, Ralph said, with that and everything else. There's no point to working, he said, if it's all a hoax. I don't know quite what to do with him. We still haven't paid his dental bill.'

What could I tell her? At that time, I believed Mother's story. 'Bring him in tomorrow, Judith. We'll have Mother issue a denial, or something. We'll figure out something. And you can have today off.'

'Thanks, Buck,' she said. 'I've a couple of stories to write first.'

'Leave your notes. I'll write 'em. I'm expecting a visitor for an important conference.'

She gave me a sheaf of typed stationery. 'These are the speeches for the Club Moderne tonight. Quote as liberally as you like. Here are the scores on the baseball game yesterday, and police notes. One drunk, two vags. Nothing ever happens in this town. See you tomorrow.'

I went out to talk to Mother Grace.

Now I want all of you *Argus* subscribers to understand that it is difficult for me to relate and interpret events from this point in my narrative to the present. I am going to be honest with you. Please believe me. But I am going to tell what I think is essential to a correct analysis, and no more. There are certain facts I must leave unrelated, for I feel that they would confuse the issue.

Newspaper reporters learn early in their training to 'slant' a story. By the twist of a phrase, by the deletion of contributing factors, they learn to make even a factual account of events in motion to mean something that is not wholly—or something that is more than—the truth. I am going to do that here, but only in order to be what I think is more honest. I want this last testament to be read and remembered as the truth.

One of the facts I am going to eliminate from consideration is the story Mother Grace had set on the Linotype while I was talking about Ralph Lake with Judith. I leave it out because it simply can't be true; I don't dare let you believe it.

When I came into the composing room, Mother added the last slug of type to the galley on his machine and took a proof. He handed it to me without comment. I read it, and I believed it—at the time.

'These are verbatim quotations from the "Sabbaticon"?' I asked.

'I'll swear to it,' Mother Grace said. 'I've been so close to that devilish book that I know it, word for word. I'll never forget it.'

I read it again. Then I followed Mother's glance to the little window high in the wall above the press. The darkness was there, too, a kind of polarised darkness which allowed light to come into the building, but prevented us from seeing out.

'I want to compare our reactions, Mother. Do you see a sort of blackness?'

'Yeah, Buck. That pencil, too. Even the hairs in my eyebrows prickled.'

'Maybe we can't get a paper out.'

'I thought about that, Buck. But let's try. We've got to let the world know.'

'Yes. We've got to let the world know. But look, if there's only one in every hundred thousand who is a Son of Satan, how could they be tracked? It would be like the seventeenth-century witch hunts. Thousands of innocents would be killed.'

'There's a sign, Buck.'

He told me the sign, and I am not telling it here, because, as I say, it would confuse the issue. And I no longer believe it.

And I ask you to believe my first statement: Dr. Evan Scot is not a Son of Satan. I ask you to take it on faith. You must believe me, as you will see. I am not going to tell you the sign so that you can look for it on him. I don't want you to become confused.

'Look, Mother,' I said as soon as I got my voice working again. 'If I can't throw a pencil through the door, it stands to reason we can't get an issue of the paper outside. But let's not shoot our whole load on an experiment. Let's put out the regular edition, with none of this in it. A trial balloon, so to speak. If that goes out, then we can shoot this tomorrow.'

'That's sense, Buck.'

'Another thing. Our—ah, visitor said he'd be back. When, do you think?'

'How the hell should I know?'

'You know more about his kind than I. You had the book, didn't you?'

That hurt him, and I hadn't meant it to. He jerked, as if I'd hit him with a lead pig, then looked at me steadily.

'Buck, if you think I'm one of the Sons that got away, and I'll admit possession of the book might indicate it, I'd rather you'd kill me here. Or I'll step out the door. I mean that, Buck. If you think there's something wrong about my ancestry, if you can't trust me to the limit, I'd rather get out. I want people to have this information, I want to help, but if you're afraid of me, I'll walk out into whatever that is waiting.'

I put my hand on his shoulder. 'Let's get to work, pal.'

That edition went out, but as you know, you didn't get a paper the next day, or yesterday. The press broke down. There was nothing unusual about it. It does that occasionally. We did not feel that supernatural forces had stopped us, because we could see a gear that had crystallised. It wasn't even dramatic, crawling around in grease and printer's ink.

But we didn't have time to talk to Judith and Ralph, and they said they'd come back later.

They did. Last night. So did the creature who had arrived while Mother Grace was chanting the paragraph from the 'Sabbaticon'. We had just finished repairing the press, cleaned ourselves up, and were having a drink, when he was suddenly there again, in the composing room with us.

His strange ears were fairly quivering. 'I've got a million things to do,' he said, 'and you pull a stupid trick like that, Grace. Shut up! Listen to me, both of you. As a result of flapping your mouth, a special reception is being prepared for you. Not only that, but I'll be forced to throw the Wall around half the houses in this town if the rumours you set in motion are accepted as facts. Fools! As if I weren't busy enough, you try to overwork me further.'

There seemed nothing to be gained by being afraid of him, or nice to him, so I said, 'You're the fool. Why did you leave that copy of the book where anybody could get it?'

'Shut up!' he snapped. 'I didn't do it. It was before my time. It wouldn't have happened if I'd had anything to do with it.'

'But it happened, and it wasn't our fault. Why should we suffer?'

'Because I say you shall.'

'So you're afraid to let the truth become known? You don't think you could cope with people if they realise that most of our eternal verities are vicious jokes to keep us unhappy forever?'

'Who said anything about truth, fool?'

'Your actions admit it. You don't have to say it.'

'I didn't say that the truth was in that book. I tell you this: the Wall is not around this building necessarily because you have discovered a truth, but because you believe it to be true. The same will be done to anyone else who believes as you.' He turned to Mother Grace, who was staring at the little window high in the wall above the press. 'Have you told this story in detail to anyone besides this idiot?'

Mother Grace was slow in bringing his eyes back into focus, and before he could say anything, a pounding rattled the locked front door, and Judith yelled:

'Oh, Buck! Let us in!'

Mother Grace answered the question. 'No. I didn't tell anybody.'

'Who's out there?' our visitor snapped.

'A couple of my employees, here for a conference.'

'Keep them in the front. I don't want them to see me. I'm busy enough as it is.'

'I'll be right back.'

I told Judith and Ralph to stay in the reception room and went back. I wanted the answer to one more question.

'Look,' I said. 'You won't admit the truth of Mother's story, you won't deny it. Answer me this: Is the "Sabbaticon" itself a hoax? Was it planted just to increase the sum total of unhappiness?'

He smiled. 'That would be an amusing refinement. If it had been planted, if people believed it, and if every man would then look on his neighbour with a suspicion of diabolic origin—yes, that would be pretty. I'll file that away for future reference.'

'Then it isn't true?'

'Oh, I didn't say that,' he said quickly. 'I didn't say anything.'

'I say the "Sabbaticon" was the hoax, then. I say that its story of the Sons of Satan was untrue. I am going to tell the readers of my paper that, if I may.'

'Surely,' he agreed. 'If you can make them believe it, I won't need to use the Wall on this town. I'll welcome anything to avoid that on top of my other duties.'

'What about us?' Mother Grace asked. 'Wh-what if w-we change our b-belief? Will we get free?'

'No. Oh, if you changed your belief, yes. But you can't. You believe it too deeply. Now, I've wasted too much time here already. I don't care what you do, but if you clear up the mess this fool started, your reception won't be quite so—ah, special, when you step into the Wall.'

He was suddenly gone, and my first sensation was regret that he had never turned his back to us once. I can't tell you whether he had a tail or not.

But I can clear up his one definite misstatement. I have said several times that I do not believe the 'Sabbaticon' was a true record. Once I had penetrated the hoax, I didn't believe any more in the Sons of Satan. My disbelief was so strong that the first thing I did was to tear up the proofs of the quotations Mother Grace had set—the quotations I did not include in this—and threw the type into the Linotype pot.

We convinced Ralph Lake. He finally believed that Mother Grace's story was a phase of D.T.'s. How we did it is not important. Those of you who know the big, stubborn prize-fighter will realise what a job we had. But he believed us, and so shall you.

Mother Grace and I also gave all our money to Judith and Ralph, and drew cheques for our bank balances, and got their promise to catch the early-morning train to Kansas City, where they will be married. I mention this here, so that the bank will honour the cheques when they come in.

* * *

The asterisks indicate an interruption. Dr. Evan Scot came in as I sat at my typewriter finishing this editorial. I don't have time to begin this over again from the beginning. Mother Grace and I are too hungry. He has been taking the sheets from me as I finish them, to set in type. This is the twenty-first sheet. I am sure you will forgive me for having used up all these words to try to prove something that was proved so dramatically a moment ago.

Mother Grace and Dr. Scot got into an argument. Dr. Scot wanted an apology. Mother Grace refused. I stepped between them to stop the fight. Mother Grace dared Dr. Scot to take off his shirt.

Mother Grace was so angry he was crying. 'You d-don't dare take it off—you don't dare, you son of Lucifer!'

Dr. Scot gave him a cold but puzzled look, and stripped slowly and deliberately to the waist. Mother Grace looked at Dr. Scot's back, and his shoulders slumped.

'I apologise, doc,' he said. 'I w-was wrong. Damn it!' he shouted, and went back into the composing room.

Dr. Scot got back into his clothes, nodded a cool goodbye to me, and stepped into the Wall. I could hear his steps on the sidewalk, but I couldn't see him, nor could I see street lamps, or star shine, through that curtain.

We are going to step into it as soon as we run this edition off the press, but I am glad there is no danger to you.

Provided—that you don't believe in the Sons of Satan. I don't. I say it again, I don't. You must not. *Must* not.

The Wall will be around your house if you do.

Here—saved until last—is undoubtedly the most sinister story you will encounter in these pages—its particular slant on our juvenile delinquents is one that only the mind of *Robert Bloch* could have devised. Bloch, who in many people's opinion is the most inventive horror story writer in the genre, has never looked back since Alfred Hitchcock's very successful screen treatment of his story 'Psycho'. Today he is kept almost constantly busy writing scripts for films and therefore new short stories are few and far between. 'Spawn of the Dark One' makes its first publication between hard covers here and will certainly chill the blood of anyone who isn't a juvenile delinquent. And those who are will get their own special kind of satisfaction from it. . . .

Spawn of the Dark One

ROBERT BLOCH

Everything was peaceful the night before the trouble came.

Ben Kerry perched on the porch rail outside his cottage, blinking like an owl in the twilight. He peered across the wide rolling expanse of the Kettle Moraine country and flapped his arms as if he were about to take off.

'There's gold in them thar hills,' he muttered. 'I never knew it, but I could have gotten in on the ground floor, too.'

Ted Hibbard grinned at him. 'You mean, when the glacier swept down and made them? You're not *that* old.'

Kerry chuckled and lit his pipe. 'That's right, son. And I wasn't here when the glacier rolled back and the Indians came, either. They used the hills for signalling posts or for their ceremonial rituals. No money in that, I grant you.'

'I know,' Hibbard said. 'I read your book about it.'

Kerry chuckled again. 'No money in *that*, either. If it wasn't for the university presses, we anthropologists would starve to death waiting for a publisher. Because we never see what's right under our noses.' He stared out at the hills again, far into deepening dusk.

'Of course the farmers didn't see, either, when they arrived here. They preferred to settle on level land. And their sons and grandsons sought still better soil, down around the waterways. So all these rock-strewn hills with their boulder outcroppings, stood deserted until maybe thirty years ago. Then the automobile brought the first hunters and fishermen from the cities. They put up cheap cabins on cheap land. And they didn't see the gold any more than I did, when I came here just before the war. All I wanted was a summer place where I could get away from people.'

Ted Hibbard chuckled, now. 'Strikes me as funny,' he said. 'An anthropologist who hates people.'

'Don't hate 'em,' Kerry insisted. 'At least, not most of 'em. Even today, you know, the majority of the inhabitants of the Earth are still savages. I've always gotten along with *them* very well. It's the civilised who frighten me.'

'Such as your students and former students?' Hibbard smiled up at him. 'I thought I was welcome here.'

'You are, believe me. But you're an exception. You aren't like the others. You don't move out here for a fast buck.'

'Oh,' Hibbard said. 'So that's what you mean by the gold, is it?'

'Of course. What you see out there isn't hill country any more. It's real estate. Development property. Right after the war the city people came. Not the hunters and the fishermen now, but the exurbanites. The super de-luxe exurbanites, who could afford to move forty miles out of town instead of just fifteen. They've been pouring in ever since, putting up their ranch-houses and their double garages for the station wagons.'

'Still looks like a pretty lonely region to me,' Hibbard mused. 'Too damned lonely, after dark.'

The Indians were afraid of the hills at night,' Kerry told him. 'They used to huddle inside their tepees around the fire. Just like today's citizens huddle inside their ranch-houses around the TV set, safe and protected.

'I suppose you have a right to be resentful,' Hibbard said. 'All these property-values going up. If you'd anticipated the boom you might have picked up choice locations years ago and made a fortune.'

Kerry shrugged. 'Wouldn't need a fortune. Just enough to move on. By now I could have a little *cabana* down along the barren stretches of the Florida Keys. I'd call it the *Key Pout*.'

A white face popped around the corner of the porch.

'Hey, Dad! Mom says it's almost time for supper.'

'Okay,' Hibbard answered. 'Tell her I'll be along soon.'

The face disappeared.

'Nice boy you have there,' Kerry said.

'Hank? We think so. Crazy about maths, all that sort of thing. Can't wait to start school in the fall. I guess he's a lot more serious about things than I was at his age. A lot more than most kids are, nowadays.'

'That's why I like him.' Kerry tapped his pipe against the porch-rail. 'You know, I'm not really such a misanthrope. This hermit pose of mine is mostly pretence. But some of it is defence, too. Defence against the mobs taking over our cities, our culture. I saw it coming, fifteen years ago. That's why I got out. It's bad enough having to stay in town during the school year, to teach. Once that's over, I come back to the cottage here. Now even this little bit of privacy is being invaded. The hot-dog stands are taking over Walden Pond, I guess.'

Hibbard stood up. 'I hope you don't resent my hanging around this way,' he said.

'Good heavens, no! When you bought your place last month I was mighty pleased to see you. I'm still a member of the human race, remember, even though I find the average rural resident as much of an alien as I do the city troglodyte or his suburbanite cousin. You're more than welcome here, at any time. I like your wife, and I like that boy of yours. They're real people.'

'Meaning that the rest are not?'

'Don't bait me,' Kerry said. 'You understand very well what I'm talking about. That's why you moved out here yourself, isn't it?'

Hibbard moved to the edge of the porch. 'Well, I guess so. Actually, we came out here because of Hank, mostly. Didn't like the city schools. Didn't like the kind of kids he ran around with back in town. They're—I don't know—different. All these juvenile delinquents. You know.'

Kerry nodded. 'Indeed I do. As a matter of fact, I've been spending most of the summer taking notes for a little monograph. Nothing pretentious, understand—sociology's out of my line—but it's an interesting study. And this happens to be an ideal spot for anthropological field-trips.'

'You mean there's a lot of rural delinquents around here?' Hibbard looked distressed. 'We were hoping to get away from that.'

'Don't worry,' Kerry reassured him. 'From what I've seen, the farm areas are still pretty well untouched. Of course, we have the usual percentage of barnyard sadists, truants, maladjusted types. But Hank won't run into too many; at his age most of them have either gone off to the armed services or the Industrial Home for Boys. It's the city youngsters I've been investigating.'

'You're talking about exurbanite kids like mine? Or is there some kind of boys' camp around here?'

'Neither. I'm speaking about our weekend visitors. Don't tell me you haven't seen them in town during the summer.'

'No, I haven't. Actually, I've been so busy getting our place straightened out that I don't get into town very often. About once a week I stock up on supplies, usually on a Wednesday. I heard it's pretty crowded, weekends.'

'You heard correctly,' Kerry told him. 'But perhaps you might be interested in seeing just what I'm talking about. I plan to take a run in, tomorrow morning, about nine or so. And you're welcome to ride along.'

'Will do.' Hibbard waved his hand in salute.

Kerry stood on the porch and watched his guest walk down the hillside path, his shoulders silhouetted against the sunset.

From the far horizon came a low, rumbling sound. It might have been the mutter of distant thunder—at least, that is what both men mistook it for at the time.

Neither of them knew that it heralded the arrival of the trouble.

They must have been coming in all through the night, and

they were still gathering around ten the following morning when Ben Kerry drove Hibbard into town in his old Ford.

Their first encounter occurred on the highway just outside the town limits, between the *Welcome To Hilltop* sign and the notice which read *Speed Limit 25 m.p.h.*

It came in the form of a rumbling again, but this time there was no mistaking it for thunder. The motorcycle roared along the road behind them, then swerved past without slackening speed. As it zoomed by, Hibbard caught a glimpse of a squat figure in a black leather jacket, with a monkey on his back. At least, it looked like a monkey in the dusty passing blur; not until a moment later did he realise that what he had seen was a girl with cropped hair who was clinging with arms entwined about the cyclist.

As they speeded ahead, Hibbard saw the girl raise her right hand as though in a gesture of greeting. Automatically he started to return her wave, then froze as Kerry gripped his shoulder.

'Look out!' he shouted, and ducked his head.

At that instant something struck the windshield of the car and bounced off with a clatter. It fell in a silvery arc to the side of the road, and Hibbard understood. The girl had not been waving. She had hurled an empty beer-can at them.

'Why, she could have broken the windshield!' he exclaimed.

Kerry nodded. 'Happens all the time. By tonight you'll find the roadside paved with empties.'

'But they aren't even supposed to *buy* beer, are they? Isn't there a state law?'

Kerry jerked his finger over his shoulder. 'Sign says you cut down to twenty-five miles an hour when you enter town, too,' he muttered. 'But they're doing close to fifty.'

'You talk as if you expected such things.'

'I do. It's like this every weekend, all summer long. Everyone knows what to expect around here.'

'And nobody tries to do anything about it?'

'Wait and see,' Kerry told him.

They were entering town now, passing a row of motels. Although it was still mid-morning, a surprising number of cars were parked before the various units. Hibbard gazed at them curiously, noting a strange incongruity. Virtually none of the vehicles were recognisable as standard units. Painted junkers, restyled hot-rods, ancient sports cars predominated. And there were dozens of motorcycles everywhere they looked.

'I see you notice our weekend visitors' choice of transportation,' Kerry said. 'I'm afraid it's apt to strike you as a bit unconventional. As a group they seem to dislike what I believe is called "Detroit iron"—you might gather from that that they utilise the motor car as a symbol of protest. As I remark in my notes, there seems to be an automotive in their madness.'

He slowed to a snail's pace as they proceeded up the short thoroughfare known, inevitably, as Main Street. The sidewalks were jammed with the usual Saturday throng of farmfolk, but intermingling with them was the unusual throng of teenage visitants.

There was no difficulty in separating them from the local youngsters; not these swaggering, guffawing figures in their metal-studded jackets and skintight jeans. Their booted feet thudded along the pavement, their visored caps bobbed. Some of them were bareheaded, choosing to display shaven skulls, crewcuts, and the more outlandish coiffures known as 'Mohawks'. An occasional older lad in the crowd was more apt to affect the other extreme; long, greasy locks and exaggerated sideburns. Several of the latter youths wore spade beards, which gave them an oddly goatish appearance. The resemblance to satyrs was perhaps increased by the presence, and the attitudes, of their female companions. Virtually all of them were indistinguishable from the girl on the motorcycle; the cropped hair, overpainted face, and tight sweater and jodhpurs seemed to be standard equipment.

Their boisterous babble rose and echoed from the artificial amphitheatre created by the store-fronts lining either side of the narrow street; from the end of the block came the sound of a juke-box blaring away at full volume inside the root-beer stand and drive-in.

A large crowd of juveniles congregated before it, and several couples were dancing on the sidewalk, oblivious of those who had to step out into the street in order to pass by. The sun's rays reflected from a score of beer-cans held in a score of hands. An orgiastic aura prevailed.

Hibbard turned to his companion. 'I think I get it now,' he said. 'I remember reading something about this a couple of years back. Wasn't there a motorcycle convention in some small town in California? A gang took over, almost started a riot?'

'There was,' the older man confirmed. 'And it happened again, last year, in another state. Then I read of another instance, this summer. If you wanted to check on such things, I imagine you'd find the phenomenon has become commonplace all over.'

'Is this what you wanted to show me?' Hibbard asked. 'That cyclist gangs are coming in here and terrorising the citizens?'

Kerry shook his head.

'Don't be melodramatic,' he murmured. 'In the first place, this isn't a "cyclist gang", any more than it's a "hot-rod crowd" or a "sports car mob" or a congregation of Elvis Presley fans. These youngsters come from all over; the big city, the outlying suburbs, the smaller industrial communities near-by. There's no outward indication that they belong to any formal group, club, or organisation. They just congregate, apparently. And if you look closely, you'll see they're not terrorising the citizens, as you put it. In fact most of the local merchants are delighted to have them here.' He waved his arm in the direction of the beer-drinkers. 'They're good customers. They leave a lot of money in town over a weekend. The sky's the limit.'

'But you said yourself that they break the laws. They must stir up trouble, get into fights, do damage.'

'They pay for it, I guess.'

'What about the local authorities? What do they think?'

Kerry smiled. 'You mean the mayor? He's a plumber here in town, gets a hundred dollars a year to hold the title as a part-time job. He doesn't worry much.'

'But the police—'

'We have a local sheriff, that's all. The place isn't even big enough to have its own jail. That's over at the county seat.'

'Don't the citizens who aren't merchants do any complaining? Are they willing to sit back and just let a bunch of strange young hoodlums run wild?'

'I guess they complain. But so far there hasn't been any action taken. For my selfish purposes, it's just as well. You'd be surprised what I've managed to observe during this summer alone. What I want to do now is get over and see one of their race meetings.'

'Race meetings?'

'That's right. You don't think they come here just to walk up and down Main Street, do you? Saturday or Sunday afternoons you'll generally find them off in the hills, on one of those little side roads back behind the county trunk highways. They rent a spot from a local farmer and hold drag races, hill-climbing contests, that sort of thing. This week there'll be a gathering in our neighbourhood, I think. They were always west of town before this, but I guess something happened and they got run off from their usual spot. Now old Lautenshlager is going to let them use the big hill behind his property. We ought to be able to see the bonfire tonight.'

'Bonfire?'

Kerry nodded. 'They usually have them.'

'What do they think they are, Indians?' Hibbard stared at a trio on the nearby corner; a skinny boy epileptically contorted over a guitar and a writhing couple who seemed to be executing an impromptu war-dance. He had to grin at the sight. 'Maybe they are, at that,' he admitted. 'They sure sound like savages.'

'Rock-and-roll,' Kerry shrugged.

Suddenly Hibbard's grin faded. 'Look at that,' he snapped, pointing up the street ahead.

A beat-up convertible was screeching down the avenue towards them, loaded with youngsters whose voices competed more than successfully with the mechanical din. As the car moved forward, a cat moved quickly out of its path. But not quickly enough, for the car swerved purposefully to the side. There was a jarring thump and a louder screech, followed by howls of laughter.

'Did you see what they did?' Hibbard demanded. 'They deliberately went out of their way to run it down! Let me out of here! I'm going to—'

'Oh, no you're not.' Kerry put his foot down on the accelerator and the Ford moved on. 'The poor thing's dead. You can't help it now. No sense starting trouble.'

'What's the matter with you?' Hibbard's voice was shrill. 'You aren't going to let them get away with this, are you?' He stared as the convertible skidded to a halt and its inmates poured out across the sidewalk. 'It's bad enough when small boys torture an animal out of childish curiosity, but these aren't children. They're old enough to know what they're doing.'

'That's right,' Kerry agreed. 'Like you say, they're savages. Remember the riots. You can't win.' Kerry drove in silence, turning off at the end of the street and cutting back along a side-road which circled the edge of town and joined the highway once again. Even at a distance it was possible to hear the blare of music, the cough of exhaust pipes, the yammer of horns and the snarl of the cycles.

'They must have noise wherever they go,' Kerry said, at last. 'I suppose it's what the psychiatrists call oral aggression.'

Hibbard didn't reply.

'Rock-and-roll is another manifestation. But then again, there was swing in your salad days and jazz in mine. In fact you can see a lot of parallels if you look for them. Eccentric dress and hair styles, the drinking—the whole pattern of rebellion against authority.'

Hibbard stirred restlessly. 'But not the senseless cruelty,' he said. 'Sure, I remember frat initiations and how wild we got after football games. But there was nothing like this. There were a few bullies or maladjusted kids with mean streaks—now they all behave like a pack of psychos.'

'Your boy isn't like that,' Kerry answered. 'Lots of them are normal.'

'Yes. But there seem to be so many of the other sort. More and more each year. Don't tell me you haven't noticed. You told me you've been studying these kids. And just now, back in town, you were afraid.'

Kerry sighed. 'Yes, I've studied them. And I am afraid.' He paused. 'How about coming home for lunch with me? I think I ought to show you a few things.'

Hibbard nodded. The noonday countryside was silent, or almost silent. It was only by listening very closely that they could hear the faint rumbling, moving along the roads in the direction of the distant hills.

Kerry spread the scrapbooks on the table after lunch. 'Started these myself some time ago,' he said. 'But recently I've signed up with a clipping service.'

He riffled the pages of the topmost book. 'Here's your motorcycle riots, and a section on gang fights. Rumbles, they call them. A report from the Police Commissioner of New York on the rise of delinquency. A list of weapons taken from a group of high school freshmen in Detroit—switchblade knives, straight razors, brass knuckles, two pistols, a hatchet. All of them used in a street battle. A section on narcotics, one on armed robbery, quite a few stories of arson. I've tried to eliminate what seem to be run-of-the-mill occurrences, so the clippings involving sex-crimes mostly concern forcible rape, gang assaults, and sadistic perversion. Even so, you can see there's a frightening assortment. This second book is devoted exclusively to news-stories of torture and murder. I warn you, it's not pleasant reading.'

It wasn't. Hibbard found his gorge rising. He'd noticed such items, of course, while skimming through his daily paper, but had never paid too much attention to their frequency. Here, for the first time, he encountered a mass accumulation, and it was an anthology of horror.

He read about the teenage kidnappers in Chicago who mutilated and then killed an infant; the youngster down South who butchered his sister; the boy who blew off the head of his mother with a shotgun. Case after case of patricide, fratricide, infanticide; instance after instance of apparently senseless slaughter.

Kerry glanced over his shoulder and sighed.

'Truth is stranger than fiction, isn't it?' he muttered. 'You'll look a long time before discovering any Penrods or Willie Baxters in those news-clippings. This isn't a Booth Tarkington world any more. For that matter, you'll search in vain for an Andy Hardy.'

'I believe it,' said Hibbard. 'But I can't understand it. Of course, there were always juvenile delinquents. Dead End Kids, that sort of thing. Only they seemed to be the exceptions, the victims of the Depression. And the zoot-suiters during the war were supposed to be the result of lack of parental supervision. The youngsters in these cases seem to be the products of normal upbringing; I notice the stories make quite a point out of the fact that most of them come from nice homes, prosperous backgrounds. So what's happened to our kids?'

'You'll still find nice children around. Hank isn't that way, remember.'

'But what's influencing the majority? Why has there been such a terrible change in the last few years?'

Kerry puffed on his pipe. 'Lots of explanations, if you want them. Dr. Wertham, for example, blames a lot of it on the comic books. Some psychotherapists say television is the villain. Others think the war left its mark; kids live in the shadow of military service, so they rebel. They've taken new heroes in their own image—James Dean, Marlon Brando, the torn-shirt totem rules their clan. Oh, there's already a most impressive literature on the subject.'

'Well, it doesn't impress me,' Hibbard declared. 'Maybe it sounds good, but how does one of those fancy theories explain a thing like this? Listen.' He jabbed his finger at one of the clippings pasted on the page opened before them. 'Here's a case from just last month. A fourteen-year-old boy, down South. He got up out of bed in the middle of the night and killed his parents in cold blood, while they slept. No rhyme or reason for it, he admits he had no reason to hate them, and the psychiatrists' reports seem to show he's perfectly normal, had an ordinary home-life. His story is that he just woke up out of a sound sleep and felt a sudden "urge to kill somebody". So he did.' Hibbard thumbed through the book. 'Come to think of it, that's what a lot of them say. They just get an "impulse", or "something comes over them", or they "want to see what it's like". And the next day the cops are beating the bushes for the bodies of missing babies, or digging up fragments of dismembered corpses in gravel-pits. I tell you, it doesn't make sense!'

He closed the scrap-book and stared at Kerry. 'You've gone to a lot of trouble to collect these clippings,' he said. 'And you say you've been studying this juvenile delinquent problem all summer. You must have come to some conclusions.'

Kerry shrugged. 'Perhaps. But I'm not quite ready to commit myself. I need further data before presenting a hypothesis.' He gave Hibbard a long look. 'You were a pretty fair student, as I recall. Let's see what you make of it all.'

'Well; there's a couple of things that occur to me. First, this insistence, in case after case, over and over again, that a youngster suddenly experiences an irresistible impulse to commit murder. Generally, in such examples, the child is alone and not part of any gang. Come to think of it, he's often an only child, isn't he, or lives an isolated life?'

Kerry's eyes narrowed. 'Go on.'

'That seems to take care of one group. But there's another—the gangs. The ones that go in for the uniforms, and the regalia. I notice there's quite a bit of referencc to initiations and secret society mumbo-jumbo. They've got a jive-talk language of their own, and fancy names, that sort of thing. And they seem to be premeditated in their crimes.' He hesitated. 'On the face of it, we're dealing with two totally different types. 'No, wait a minute—there's one thing all these kids seem to have in common.'

Kerry leaned forward. 'What's that?'

'They don't *feel* anything—no shame, no guilt, no remorse. There's no empathy towards their victims, none at all. Time after time the stories bring that point out. They kill for kicks, but it doesn't really touch them at all. In other words, they're psychopaths.'

'Now we're getting somewhere,' Kerry said. 'You call them psychopaths. And just what *is* a psychopath?'

'Why, like I said—somebody who doesn't have normal feeling, who lacks responsibility. You've studied up on psychology, you ought to know.'

Kerry gestured towards the row of bookshelves lining the sides of his fireplace. 'That's right. I've got quite a collection of psychotherapy texts up there. But you can search through them in vain for a satisfactory definition of the so-called psychopathic personality. He isn't considered a psychotic. He doesn't respond to any form of treatment. No psychiatric theory presently offers a demonstrable explanation of how a psychopath evolves, and for lack of contrary evidence it's often assumed that he's born that way.'

'Do you believe that?'

'Yes. But unlike orthodox therapists, I have a reason. I think I know what a psychopath is. And—'

'Dad!'

Both of them turned at the cry.

Hibbard's son stood in the doorway, the rays of the late afternoon sun reflecting redly from the bright blood streaming down the side of his face.

'Hank! What happened? Did you have an accident?' He moved towards the boy.

'No, I'm all right. Honest I am. I just didn't want to go home and scare Mom.'

'Sit down.' Kerry led him to a chair. 'Let me get some hot water, clean you off.' He went over to the sink and returned with a cloth and a basin. Skilfully he sponged the blood away, revealing the lacerations on the scalp.

'Not too deep,' he told Hibbard. 'A little peroxide and a bandage, now.'

The boy winced, then subsided as Kerry finished his ministrations.

'Better?'

'I'm all right,' Hank insisted. 'It's just that they hit me with the tyre-chain—'

'Who hit you?'

'I don't know. Some guys. I went for a walk this afternoon, and I heard all this racket up on the hill behind old Lautenshlager's place, you know. And I saw all these guys, and some dames, too. They were riding motorcycles up and down, making a lot of noise. I wanted to see what was going on, that's all, I just wanted to see what was going on—'

His lower lip trembled and Hibbard patted his shoulder. 'Sure, I understand. So you went up there, eh? And then what happened?'

'Well, I started to go up. But before I could get very close, these big guys jumped me. There must have been five or six of them, they just came out from around some bushes and grabbed me. And one of them had a stick and another one had this tyre-chain, and he swung it at me and hit me alongside of the head, here. The others let go of me to get out of the way, and that's how I got loose. I started to run, and they were chasing me, only I got across the fence and then I ducked down behind Lautenshlager's barn so they couldn't see me.'

'Did you get a good look at the fellows?'

'Well, one of them had a beard. And they were all wearing these black leather jackets and some kind of boots.'

'It's the gang, all right. Our friends, the psychopaths.' Hibbard stood up. 'You can walk, can't you? Then come on.'

'Where are we going?'

'Home, of course. I'm going to see to it that you get to bed. You got quite a knock, there. And then I think I'll hop in the car and take a little run over to the county seat. Seems to me this is a matter for the state police.'

Kerry put down his pipe. 'Are you sure it's wise to stir up trouble?' he asked, quietly. 'No telling what might happen.'

'Something has happened already,' Hibbard answered. 'When a bunch of hoodlums knock my son over the head with a tyre-chain, that's trouble enough for me. Come on, Hank.'

He led the boy out of the door and down the path, without a backward look.

Kerry grimaced, then shook his head. For a moment he opened his mouth to call after them, then closed it. After that he just stood there, his eyes intent on the far hills. No smoke rose from them in the waning horizon-light, but the sound of racing exhausts was plainly audible. Kerry stood there listening for a long time. Then, slowly, wearily, he walked into the front room. He kindled a fire in the fireplace and sat down before it, balancing a notebook on his lap. From time to time he scribbled a few words, sitting stiffly, head poised as though listening for an unexpected sound. His face bore the tight, strained look of a man who had been waiting for trouble—and found it. He concentrated deeply.

It must have been almost an hour before the sound came. Even though he'd been tensed and alert, Kerry jumped when he heard the footsteps. He rushed to the door, reaching it just as Hibbard burst in.

'Oh, it's you!' His voice rose in relief. 'So dark I didn't recognise who it was at first.'

Hibbard didn't respond for a moment. He stood there, panting, waiting to regain his breath.

'Ran all the way,' he wheezed.

'What's the matter? Is it Hank?'

'No. The kid's all right, I guess. We put him to bed when I got him home, and my wife doesn't think there's any concussion. She used to be a nurse, you know. So I decided to grab a sandwich before I drove in for the police. We had the door shut, so I guess that's why I didn't hear anything. They must have sneaked in and out of the yard again very quietly. My wife didn't hear them either.'

'Who?'

'Our young friends. Guess they figured out where Hank lived and decided I might be going after them. Anyway, they weren't taking any chances. They slashed all my tyres.'

Hibbard's voice rose. 'They could see there are no telephone wires around our place, and I suppose they thought if they fixed the car I couldn't do anything. But I'll show them!'

'Take it easy, now.'

'I am taking it easy. I'm just here to borrow your car, that's all.'

'You still intend to get the police?'

'What do you mean, *still*? After what just happened, nothing could stop me. I made sure everything was locked good and tight when I left, but even that's no guarantee. For all I know, they'll be around to burn the house down before the night is over.'

Kerry shook his head. 'I don't think so. I think if you just go back home and stay there quietly there won't be any more trouble. All they want now is to be left alone.'

'Well what they want and what they're going to get are two different things. I'm going to round up every police officer, every trooper in this part of the state. We're going to put an end to this sort of thing—'

'No. You won't end it. Not that way.'

'Look, I'm not here to argue with you. Give me your car-keys.'

'Not until you listen to me, first.'

'I listened to you long enough. I should have got tough the minute I saw those kids run over the cat.' Hibbard wiped his forehead. 'All right, what is it you wanted to say?'

Kerry walked over and stood next to the bookshelves.

'We were talking about psychopaths this afternoon. I told you that psychiatrists didn't understand them, but that I did. Sometimes it takes an anthropologist to know these things. In my time I've studied a great deal concerning the so-called "gang-spirit" and the secret societies of many cultures. You find them in all regions, and there are certain similarities. For example, did you know that in some places, even the young women have their own groups? Lips says—'

'I'm not interested in a lecture.'

'You will be. Lips says there are hundreds of such societies in Africa alone. The Bundu group, in Nigeria, wears special masks and costumes for their secret rituals. The male adventurer who dares to spy on them is disciplined, or even killed.'

'Listen, a gang of crazy kids around a bonfire isn't any secret lodge!'

'You noted the similarity yourself, this afternoon.'

'I said some kids ran in gangs, yes. But others don't. What about the "loners", the ones who just get the urge to kill?'

'They don't know what they are, that's all. They haven't recognised themselves. For that matter, I don't think the gangs do, not consciously. They think they are just out for thrills. And I only pray that they go on that way, that they don't realise what brings them together.'

'We know what brings them together. They're all a bunch of psychos.'

'And what *is* a psychopath?' Kerry's voice was soft. 'A psychotherapist couldn't tell you, but an anthropologist can. A psychopath is a fiend.'

'What?'

'A fiend. A devil. A creature known in all religions, at all times, to all men. The spawn of a union between a demon and a mortal woman.' Kerry forced a smile. 'Yes, I know how it sounds. But think a moment. Think of when all this started—this wave of sudden, unnatural juvenile crime, of psychopathic cruelty. Only a few years ago, wasn't it? Just about the time when the babies born in the early years of the war started to enter their teens. Because that's when it happened, during the war, when the men were away. And the women had nightmares—the kind of nightmares some women have had throughout the ages. The nightmare of the incubus, the carnal demon who visits them in sleep. It happened before in the history of our culture, during the Crusades. And then followed the rise of the witch-cults all over Europe—the witch-cults presided over and attended by the spawn of the night-fiends; the half-human offspring of a blasphemous union. Don't you see how it all fits into the pattern? The unholy love of cruelty for its own sake, the strange, sudden maniacal urge to torture and destroy which comes in sleep, the hideous inability to respond to normal sentiment and normal feelings, the seemingly irrational way in which certain youngsters are irresistibly drawn together into groups who thrive on violence? As I said, I don't think that even the gangs realise the truth about themselves yet—but if they ever do, you'll see a wave of Satanism and Black Magic which will put the Middle Ages to shame. Even now, they gather about fires in the summer night, seeking the hilltop haunts—'

'You're batty!' Hibbard grabbed Kerry by the shoulder and shook him roughly. 'They're just kids, that's all. What they need is a damned good beating, the whole lot of them, and maybe a couple of years in reform school.'

Kerry shook him off. 'Now you're talking like the authorities—the truant officers and the police and the get-tough school of welfare workers. Don't you see, that's just the way they've tried to handle the problem, and it never works? Any more than psychotherapy can work? Because you're dealing with something you're no longer conditioned to believe in. You're dealing with fiends. What we need is exorcism. I can't let you go up there, tonight. The police will just start a riot, it will be murder—'

Hibbard hit him, then, and he went down. His head struck the edge of the fireplace and he lay silent, an ugly bruise rising along the side of his right temple. Hibbard stooped, felt his pulse, then gasped in relief. Quickly he explored the contents of Kerry's jacket-pockets. His hands closed over the car-keys.

Then he rose, turned, and ran from the cottage.

Kerry came to with a start. There was a throbbing in his head. He grasped the mantel, pulled himself erect. The throbbing intensified. But it wasn't all in his head; part of it pounded in rhythm from a distance. He recognised the sound, the roaring that came from the hills.

He rubbed his forehead, then walked slowly in the direction of the porch. The distant darkness was dissolved in a reddish glow, and he could see the flames rising now from the far hill-top.

Kerry felt in his pockets, then swore and started for the door. He hesitated in the doorway, then returned to the living-room and stooped over his desk. His hand scrabbled in the right top drawer; closed over a small revolver. He slipped it into his jacket-pocket and headed for the door once again.

It was dark on the path, but the faint flicker of flames guided his descent. When he reached the bottom of the hill and made sure that his car was gone, he swore again, then squatted until he discerned the fresh tyre-tracks and the direction in which they led. Hibbard had chosen to take the back road, the nearest approach to the highway which led to the county seat. The road was rough and it skirted directly behind the big hill on the Lautenshlager property, but it would be the fastest route. Kerry wondered if he'd reach the highway in time to head off the police. He hadn't been able to convince Hibbard, but he was willing to try again. The police weren't going to solve the situation. There'd just be more violence. If he only had time to work on the problem *his* way, to talk to those who still retained faith in the age-old remedy of exorcism, the casting-out of demons—

Kerry lengthened his stride, smiling wryly to himself. He couldn't blame Hibbard for his reaction. Most men were of the same mind today. Most *civilised* men—that is to say, the small minority of our western culture who go their way blindly, ignoring the other billion and a half who still know, as they have always known, that the forces of darkness exist and are potent. Potent, and able to spawn.

Perhaps it was just as well they didn't believe. He'd told Hibbard the truth—the only immediate hope lay in the fact that the changelings themselves weren't entirely aware of their own nature. The fiends didn't know they were fiends. Once they came to learn, and united—

He put the thought away as he worked around behind the hill where the fire flared. Kerry sought the shadows at the side of the road for concealment; the noise of racing motors and the sound of shouts muffled his passing.

Then he rounded a sharp turn and saw the car looming drunkenly in the ditch. Through narrowing eyes he recognised the vehicle as his own. Had there been an accident? He started forward, calling softly. 'Hibbard—where are you?'

The figure emerged from the edge of darkness. 'Kind of thought you'd be along.'

Kerry had just time enough to wonder about the oddly altered voice; time enough for that and no more. Because then they were all around him, some of them holding and some of them striking, and he went down.

When he came to he was already on top of the hill; yes, he must be, because the big brush-fire was leaping and roaring right before him, and the figures were leaping and roaring around it.

Why it was like the old woodcuts, the ones showing the Sabbat and the Adoration of the Master. Only there was no

Master in the centre of the fire—just this burned and blackening figure, a charred dummy of some sort, thrust upright against a post. And the youngsters were dancing and capering, somebody was plucking the guts of a guitar, it was rock-and-roll, just a gang of kids having a good time. Some of them were drinking beer and a few had even started up their motorcycles to race in a circle about the flames.

Sure, they'd panicked and hit him, but they were only teenagers, he told himself, it had to be that way. And he'd explain, he'd tell them. He had to thrust the other thought from his mind, had to. Now they were pulling him into the circle and the big kid, the one with the beaver-tails dangling from his cap, was grinning at him.

'We found the other one,' he called. 'Clobbered him before he got away.'

'Man, he's all shook up.'

'Must be hip. He was on his way to town.'

'If he got there, we'd really have a gasser.'

'Ungood.'

'What'll it be?'

Kerry whirled, seeking the source of the voices. He stared at the circle of goatish, grinning faces in the firelight. A girl danced past, bop-fashion, her eyes wild.

'How about the sacrifice bit?'

And then they were all shouting. 'The sacrifice bit, that's it! Yeah, Man!'

Sacrifice. Man. The *Black Man* of the Sabbat.

Kerry fought the association, he had to fight it, he couldn't believe that. And then they were pushing him closer to the fire, and he could see the blackened dummy.

When he recognised what was burning there he couldn't fight the knowledge any more, and it was too late to fight the hands which gripped him, held him, then thrust him forward into the flames.

A mighty shout went up and he made one last effort to retain his faculties. If only he could hear what they were screaming—at least then he'd learn the final truth. *Did they or did they not know what they really were?*

But he fell forward, fainting, as the motorcycles began to race around the fire.

Their roaring drowned out every other sound, so even at the end, Kerry never heard the chanting.

Black Magic Battle in Church
Three Satanists fight Vicar, 78

Satanists last night fought a seventy-eight-year-old vicar in his peaceful, country church.

It happened in the chancel of the twelfth century parish church at Westham, Sussex.

The devil worshippers were discovered in the middle of a Black Magic ritual by church bellringer Walter Binsted.

He saw them chanting around lighted candles which had been put on the floor in the shape of a cross. Two of the candles had been taken from the altar.

Mr. Binsted ran to the village school next door, where a church fete was being held, to fetch help.

Then he rushed back to the church with the vicar, the Rev. Harold Coulthurst, the churchwarden, Captain Leo Hayden, 65, and parishioners, Bob Tourle and Reginald Wood.

A fight broke out as they tried to detain the three men. One man was knocked down and Captain Hayden's glasses were sent flying.

But the men escaped. They ran to a blue and grey car, parked near Pevensey Castle, 600 yards away, and roared off.

Mr. Binsted, of Battle Road, Westham, said 'I saw a light in the church belfry and wondered who could be there.

'When I turned on the lights in the church, I saw men doing a kind of mumbo jumbo chant.'

The vicar said *'I have no doubt that this was one of the Black Magic gangs we have been warned about. They have lit fires and desecrated churches in Somerset.*

'We grabbed them, but they were to strong for us. They fought their way to the church door and ran to their car.'

Late last night, police patrols were hunting the men. All are aged about thirty.

Police said there was also evidence that the men had spat at the altar cross.

Sunday Mirror
December 8th, 1968

ACKNOWLEDGEMENTS

The editor is grateful to the following authors, their agents and publishers, for permission to include copyright material in this book: Messrs. Hutchinson Ltd. for 'The Satanic Mass' by Montague Summers, 'The Sanctuary' by E. F. Benson and 'The Black Magician' by Dennis Wheatley; The Scott Meredith Literary Agency for 'The Festival' by H. P. Lovecraft and 'The Watcher from the Sky' by August Derleth; B.P. Singer Features for 'Spawn of the Dark One' by Robert Bloch; Messrs. A. P. Watt & Son for 'Ancient Sorceries' by Algernon Blackwood; Messrs. A. D. Peters for 'The Book' by Margaret Irwin; Cleve Cartmill for his story 'No News Today'; and the executors of the Estate of Aleister Crowley for 'The Initiation'. Particular thanks are also extended to August Derleth and Paul Tabori for their many favours during the compiling of this book.

P.H.